Dear Agi

M

You much מזל and much
נחת, now and always with
Tibi and your 2 special sons–

love,

Shire

50
Pathways to
PARENTING
WISDOM

50
Pathways to
PARENTING
WISDOM

Shira Frank, LCSW

Introduction by **Rebbetzin Tziporah Heller**

ISBN 978-1-60091-282-5

Page layout and design: E. Chachamtzedek

DISTRIBUTED BY:
Israel Bookshop Publications
501 Prospect Street
Lakewood, NJ 08701

Tel: (732) 901-3009
Fax: (732) 901-4012
www.israelbookshoppublications.com
info@israelbookshoppublications.com

Printed in the United States

This book is dedicated to
my beloved parents

Dov (Ben) ז"ל

and

Sarah Rivkah (Sylvia) עמו"ש
Silvers

They dedicated their lives to spreading
goodness and kindness to others.

May my siblings and our families
continue to learn from their example.

Without question, the greatest challenge people face is "successful parenting." The traditions and practices that formed the framework in the shtetl are gone, and the high-tech, instant-gratification of our culture requires special techniques to raise healthy, productive, happy and respectful children.

Shira Frank has provided us with fifty techniques, stated concisely and clearly, to help us meet this awesome challenge of modern life.

Rabbi Abraham J. Twerski, MD

David Pelcovitz, Ph.D.

Professor, Straus Chair in Psychology and Education
Azrieli Graduate School of Jewish Education
and Administration, Yeshiva University

Shira Frank has written a highly practical guide to parenting our children in an increasingly complex world. Informed by decades of practice as a therapist helping parents strike the delicate balance between love and limits, this book presents easily implemented approaches to raising children through use of praise, empathy and an unemotional and gentle strategy for limit setting.

In addition to suggesting practical, Torah-informed strategies for improving communication, Mrs. Frank tackles special challenges such as helping children deal with divorce, and providing guidance for parents faced with the unique stress of parenting children with special conditions such as Attention Deficit Disorder, anxiety disorders or Pervasive Developmental Disorder.

Shira Frank has provided our community with an invaluable resource for helping parents navigate the increasingly complex demands of raising children. I highly recommend this book.

Dr. David Pelcovitz

Contents

Communication Techniques

Teaching Children Coping Mechanisms

Self-Esteem Issues

Children — Specific Behavioral Challenges

Parents' Emotional Responses to Their Children

Introduction

by Rebbetzin Tziporah Heller

ONCE THERE WAS a time in which we parents had little option but to do our best to observe the best parenting available to us. Sometimes we were fortunate enough to come from wonderful families who live what parenting books teach. Sometimes we weren't. We were living in times that were different than those of the generations preceding us. Some of our parents were Holocaust survivors — some of whom had to do their best at parenting, while living with scars that neither could, nor would heal. Some of us were *baʾalei teshuvah*, newcomers to Judaism, who had no model of what a Torah family looks like and how it functions.

Many books were written to fill the gap, and some of them have rightly become classics. One problem that arises all too often is that some of the writers applied what they learned in the secular arena to this very unique aspect of Jewish life. While we all know the *Midrashic* adage: "Believe that the nations have wisdom, but don't believe that they have Torah," we don't always realize what the implication of this dictum is. And when the topic under discussion is not "how to build a computer," but rather how to raise a child, it is a different story. A Jewish child is destined to be more than just happy, well-adjusted and productive. He is meant to be a light source, and that can only happen if he is fortunate enough to believe that he has light to shed. By the nature of things, a secularly inspired book cannot address the spiritual needs and aspirations of the Jewish family. There are other books in which the ideals of "*chinuch al taharas hakodesh*," pure undiluted parenting and teaching are described and idealized. The problem is that the goals are noble and valid, but the methods are either difficult to put into practice in today's world, or not presented with the sort of clarity that today's rather clueless parents yearn to have.

Shira Frank's book is an authentic guide book for parents raising kids in today's world. Her ideas may be useful and sometimes make all the difference in changing and building a positive relationship between parents and children. Mrs. Frank's theories have been tested by decades of experience in the Torah-observant community. The sort of skill that she has taught parents for years is the method of taking the value of judging favorably and applying this to *chinuch*, without self-deception. I have known Shira Frank for decades, and am a dear friend. She has made an extremely valuable contribution to the world of *chinuch* through the pages of this book.

Foreword

THERE ARE MANY pathways to wisdom, and one needs to have *siyatta diShmaya* (the assistance from Heaven) to find the appropriate path to take when dealing with one's child. It is said that all the *sha'arim* (gates) of Heaven are closed, except that of tears. Through our own sincere self-searching and introspection, may we come to find the gate to our children's hearts.

In general, the ideas in this book have been compiled from human encounters in the realm of social work, spanning over a thirty-year period of time. The parenting ideas mentioned are realistic, not reflecting one parenting philosophy alone, but rather focusing on practical ideas that many parents have found to be helpful.

As parents in the 21st century are confronted with new challenges, creative parental responses to these challenges need to emerge. Parental responses that may have been resourceful and helpful thirty years ago do not necessarily speak to the present reality of our society.

Perhaps the main difference apparent among youth, reflecting our present society, is that of the availability of an abundance of information and openness to the society-at-large that has never occurred in the American Jewish community. The touch of a button on the computer gives a person access to many worlds that may never have been explored. Though their glimmer may be artificial and transitory, they capture the minds of youth — *mayim genu-vim yimtaku* — "Whatever is forbidden seems sweet and desirable."

On a practical level, when a child's *rebbi* seems severe and unrelenting in the classroom, a student can always compare him to the kind and gentle man on the computer, who seems to continually have patience and shows warmth. Though media-visitation reflects an artificial time-limited vision of humane individuals, children are often enamored with such characters (i.e. baseball players, entertainers).

Thus, parents and educators need to be more positive and non-judgmental in response to children, reflecting Torah sources of "*yad yemin mekareves*" (the right hand brings closer), through kindness. While "*yad smol docheh*" (the left hand pushes away), to clarify what is negative behavior, the initial response to children is by using the "*yad yemin*" (the right hand). The "left hand" of severity is not the initial response to any individual. If a person knows about the *mitzvah* and avoids it, the person is only more culpable as it is now *b'meizid*. Thus, we are not necessarily helping a person by being forceful in our opinion (even if we are right).

On the other hand, learning consequences of one's actions is of utmost importance in the *chinuch* of a child. If a child does not realize that problematic behavior will yield a negative consequence, he will be continually disappointed in his life. He will question why he is unable to maintain friendships, or why his teacher is irritated with him. Thus, "time-out" and some sort of punishment is often necessary to establish societal guidelines. Oppositional and impulsive children often need to see these guidelines continually.

However, giving consequences to children alone does

not modify problematic behavior. Consequences are a type of reality testing, for children and adults. "B" will occur if you do "A."

In reality, positive verbal statements and actual rewards prove to be the most effective motivator in bringing improvement to a child's patterns of behavior. If we look honestly into our own characters, we will find this to be true within ourselves as well. If we envision whatever achievements we have managed to accrue in our lifetimes, weren't they usually motivated by positive encouragement and belief in ourselves, rather than fear and being forced to achieve?

The parenting ideas mentioned throughout this book reflect general family experiences, besides more specific issues that are unique to individual families. Topics such as PDD and divorce are touched upon, reflecting the gamut of possible family challenges. Each category is not meant to be an extensive response to the complex topic discussed, but rather a direction to strive for in a very difficult circumstance. Professional help should always be sought when circumstances become too overwhelming and a more specific direction needs to be taken. It is not a poor reflection upon parents if a "new highway is too difficult to navigate." May Hashem make the task of *gidul banim* have decreased *tzaar*, and increased *simchah*, on a day-to-day basis.

Shira Frank LCSW, 2013

Acknowledgments

IN THE WINTER of 2006, my fifteen-year-old son Menachem was the initial inspiration which led to the creation of this book. My son asked that I purchase a computer program which would tape him reading into the computer, in order that he would be able to read my published "self-help" articles into the computer. In this way, he felt that eventually a book would be published.

Though this job became much more complicated (especially with the Hebrew vocabulary not being understood by the computer), Menachem's continual interest in this endeavor started this process several years ago. Many thanks goes to his siblings, Liba, Elisheva, their spouses and children, and Aharon, Moshe, and Devorah for being helpful in many ways in various stages of this book's inception.

In truth, a great part of the spiritual inspiration of this book comes from my husband Avraham, who continually gives to all of us and to all of *Klal Yisrael*. May Hashem continually give him the strength to do his *avodas hakodesh*.

Much thanks for my mother's continual editing of my articles over the years, and for the unlimited contribution of unconditional love that she shows towards all of my family.

I owe a very special thanks to my devoted and truth-seeking brother Dean Silvers, his wife Marlen, and their most special family. My brother's input and support on every level has made a qualitative difference in my life.

And a special thanks to my wonderful oldest brother Marc Silvers, whose caring and kind nature are a gift to all those who know him.

With special thanks to my most dear friend Shulamis Kaplinsky, whose clarity of vision and endless capacity of compassion towards others is a continual inspiration to me and to so many others. Her words, thoughts and encouragement help the author and so many others, continually.

Special thanks to Dr. David Pelcovitz, who was my first colleague who reviewed the manuscript. His comments and interest helped spearhead the writing of this book.

After many painstaking hours of working on editing and proofreading this book, Mrs. Tzippora Zaslow, who is on the editorial staff of *Hamodia* and *Binah*, was successful in putting together my manifold thoughts in a way that I feel confident that my message has come across clearly.

With much thanks to Eden Chachamtzedek, my typesetter, whose sincere and skilled concern for each detail in the book helped my work to be a labor of love, rather than an arduous trial of details.

In relation to graphic design, Yisroel Lipshitz's initial photograph beautifully reflects the book's message. Shevy Appel continued this idea, expanding on the theme of the book in its lovely cover.

Without a doubt, the direction and structure of this book has taken on its final form through the expertise and great patience of Liron Delmar of Israel Bookshop Publications. Her humility and creative ideas has made this journey a most pleasant one!

A most special *hakaras hatov* to Harav Shmuel Kamenetsky, whose support and encouragement of the printing of this book leaves a great imprint on all of us. The Rosh Yeshivah is truly a living example of the exemplary character traits that are mentioned in this book.

I thank *Hakadosh Baruch Hu* for the opportunity to work with so many special individuals who attempt to help accelerate growth on an emotional and spiritual level through daily human encounters.

Shira Frank,
28 Tishrei 5774

TALMUDICAL YESHIVA OF PHILADELPHIA

6063 Drexel Road
Philadelphia, Pennsylvania 19131
215 - 477 - 1000

Rabbi Elya Svei
Rabbi Shmuel Kamenetsky
Roshei Yeshiva

50 Pathways to Parenting Wisdom is an enlightening collection of practical ideas for good parenting. The fact that this little book is very concise is a further enhancement for busy parents to read and learn from. The author, Shira Frank, provides the tools which will benefit parents and children alike. May Hashem grant her much success in helping כלל ישראל.

Shmuel Kamenetsky

COMMUNICATION TECHNIQUES

The "cushion method" — pleasant communication techniques

1

R ABBI AKIVA DESCRIBED the great difficulty that we all have in receiving rebuke from one another many hundreds of years ago, in *Eruvin* (16). Our spiritual condition in this area does not seem to have improved greatly over the many generations. Conveying negative or critical information to one's child (or to anyone) is a difficult task, as both the giver and the receiver are in an uncomfortable position. However, if the information is imparted in a more sensitive manner, the recipient may feel less of a sense of confrontation and belittlement. One way to envision this idea is to imagine two soft pillows before you, and in between these two pillows is the actual critical comment that is necessary to be stated.

The initial "soft pillow" of communication can consist of: a) a statement giving the benefit of the doubt, such as: "I'm sure that you were unaware of this, but…" or b) a statement reflecting your need to clarify information, such as: "I think I may have misunderstood something, so I need you to help me out…"

After such sensitivity shown in such a dialogue, one can more easily insert words of necessary negativity before inserting the "second pillow" of comforting words. As one is already in a mindset of being more sensitive, the actual critical statement will be said in a softer tone, with more compassion and kindness.

The "second pillow" reflects words of comfort, and shows how one believes in the capabilities of the person. The Rambam speaks of the need for a person who is angry to give the accused a chance to do *teshuvah* by believing in his ability to change and rectify his deeds. In a similar vein, one's "second pillow" shows belief in the problematic issue being rectified in the present or in the near future. An example of such a statement might be: "I know that this was unintentional, and I am sure that there is a way that we can work this out." In this manner, a person (a child particularly) will feel less attacked, and be more willing to actually listen to the information being imparted.

2 Getting quiet kids to talk — "mutual storytelling"

IN THE *GEMARA* in *Sanhedrin*, the decision to speak to others, or refraining from speaking to others when upset by life's disappointments, is discussed. The language used in the *Gemara* is: *Da'agah b'lev ish, yasichenu lacheirim* (When there are worries in the heart of man, speak/hide it from others). There are occasions when it is meritorious to speak to others when upset, as reflected when the word "*yasichenu*" is written with a *sin*, reflecting "*siach*," the word speech. There are also other times when it is better that a person keeps these feelings to himself, as reflected when the word "*yasiach*" is written with a *samech*, reflecting "*hesech*" (the word reflecting a state of hiding). At times, speaking about worries may only aggravate the situation. Clearly, there are times when children (and adults) need time to think and introspect without the help of others.

However, when a child barely communicates with his parents, techniques need to be applied to assist this situation. A parent first needs to analyze the general relationship between parent and child and see if any particular aspect of this relationship needs improvement. Perhaps a parent may be too critical or sarcastic towards a child, or is a mediocre listener when his child speaks to him. Perhaps a child's opinions are being devalued, or other siblings' voices are overshadowing this child. A parent may continually bring up a topic that is irritating to a child, etc. Before a parent attempts "mutual storytelling," he needs first to look at the quality of dialogue between parent and child, and see if there is room for improvement.

If a child generally responds monosyllabically (saying only "yes" or "no") to a parent, he needs to attempt to create more of an atmosphere of trust with this child. If a child seems to be troubled about something, and a parent is not sure of the exact nature of the problem, asking a child many direct questions is often unhelpful. What may be helpful is approaching the issue in a more indirect manner. A parent may guess the nature of the issue that the child is involved with and attempt to relate a similar situation experienced by the parent in his childhood. By speaking to his child about a past childhood experience and sharing his feelings about this experience, a child feels that his pain is shared. Even if a child shrugs his shoulders or says: "That's not what's happening to me," at least he sees his parent's desire to reach out and be empathetic. He might even say:

"That's not what is happening to me — but, THIS is what is going on."

A child is often less embarrassed to tell about his own circumstance, after his parent showed his own vulnerability. He may also feel less uncomfortable with not being "perfect," and not fearful that he will disappoint his parents by his lack of perfection. The concept that I'm describing has been coined "mutual storytelling" — by telling our "story," we hope to elicit responses from our children, and hear their "story." At times, the actual way that the problem was (or was not) resolved by a parent can shed light and insight on a child's problematic situation. This communication technique has proven to be very effective in building new bridges of communication between parent and child.

3 *Three sympathetic and reflective statements which are helpful in communicating with your children*

PARENTS SOMETIMES CANNOT find the words to reflect a child's feelings. However, certain statements can help a child to feel more comfortable in expressing emotion. Examples of this might be: "Wow. I can imagine how hard that might have been," or "I remember very well what that feels like," or "That really is a lot to happen in one day." Being sympathetic and reflective helps builds the relationship between parent and child, allowing for trust and understanding to grow.

TEACHING
CHILDREN
COPING
MECHANISMS

Stress giving the benefit of the doubt — decreasing anger and resentment

4

THOUGH WE ARE told the great merit of giving another the benefit of the doubt, the actual ability to do so and actually believe the thought that we are attempting to put in our mind is far from simple. We are often so consumed with anger and resentment that this judging "*l'chaf zechus*" seems to be more of a "lip service" than the service of the heart. Yet, so often we find that there are mitigating circumstances that caused the situation to unfold as it did, and our given theory of the situation was indeed inaccurate. Our anger and disappointment was unwarranted, and in relation to our role as a parent, we see that not giving the benefit of the doubt only increases mistrust between parent and child.

Sometimes (clearly not in all situations), it is better to believe in one's child, even if one doubts the total truth of his statements, in order to build a relationship with the child. Often, verbally doubting much of what a child says becomes a belittling match. As stated in relation to doubting people's sincerity, a person needs to "*kabdeihu v'chashdeihu*" (respect him and suspect him). In certain circumstances with one's children, one can even verbalize this dilemma: "I understand your explanation of this situation. It does make sense. However, I see other things happening here that you may not even been thinking of...." This is usually more preferable than: "Do you think that I was born yesterday? I know how you're trying to paint this story, so that I'll give you the car again." The second response generally only creates a power struggle, where both parent and child do not want to be seen as "the fool." As stated in *Mishlei*, "It is better to be deemed as a fool than to go against the dictates of Hashem."

Creating a relationship of trust between parent and child allows true *chinuch* to occur. If there is limited trust, the transmission of our *mesorah* can barely exist between parent and child, as the main encounters become those of power struggles and strife. Again, if such encounters are a frequent occurrence, the communication between parent and child needs to change. There is more of a need for *gevurah* (and more words of severity) in such circumstances, but the words still need to be couched with caring and belief in one's child's continual potential to be successful. *Chazal* stress the great importance of this idea: *Hama'avir al middosav, mochlin al kol pesha'av* (Whoever forgives a person's bad character traits, Hashem forgives all of his sins). If one believes in the ultimate *kedushah* and good of people, Hashem will see only the good within him.

5   *Teaching your children understanding and compassion towards authority*

A S THE YEARS progress, parents' concerns are about their children's teachers and friends and about how their children are acclimating to their learning and social situation. Parents sometimes think that a particular teacher would be very advantageous for their child, but they may be incorrect in their assumptions. Parents may also be keenly concerned about their teenage children's teachers, as these children look for hypocrisy in adults and have no tolerance for adults whose philosophy and actions are inconsistent with each other (though they have much tolerance for their own inconsistencies).

In order to have more understanding of our children's teachers, we need to envision the typical life of teachers. Many of us could not tolerate working at a job that does not pay us in a timely fashion. Utility companies and tuition committees have payment deadlines and make that clear to their consumers. Teachers cannot necessarily pay on time, since they are not paid on time, so they are often under stress to pay the many bills that maintaining a family entails.

In the past it was said that if a person couldn't do any other job, he could always teach. In our present society, this adage is no longer accurate. Many who leave *kollel* greatly desire a good teaching position with "normative children," but that is a rarity. The market is quite competitive.

Generally, those who teach want to do so. It is true that many who want to teach are poorly trained and have limited talent, and that causes many problems in our schools. It is also true that maintenance of many schools is such a financial burden that in-service training for teachers on a continual basis becomes a luxury. Thus we find ourselves in a situation with many limitations.

Another issue difficult to resolve is that of unskilled teachers remaining in school systems for many years. Though parents rightfully resent this, the options are limited.

Public and certain private schools give their teachers tenure in order to give them job security. No teacher wants to look for a new school or new grade yearly, as much preparation is involved in preparing for a new class and school. Therefore, yeshivos have somewhat of an informal tenure system. If they did not, the amount of teachers seeking employment would be reduced. Also, when principals evaluate teachers and classes, they often get a non-realistic view, as classes and teachers are on their best behavior when the principal enters the classroom.

Once a parent and student understand and learn to tolerate the limitations of the teaching profession in our yeshivos, they need to learn to tolerate their own personal limitations. When a person finds fault with and is irritated by another's character flaw, that flaw actually exists within the person himself, according to the Baal Shem Tov. That is why the person finds the character trait so bothersome; he has to live with the very same limitation.

If the character trait of a teacher is very bothersome to a student, the parent can stress the idea that a student can learn from all types of personalities. Eventually one may have a rigid boss or relative that one needs to learn to deal with, so learning to deal with such a person is a learning experience for one's future. Clearly we would not choose this challenge for our children, but we cannot continually change classes for our children every year if the teacher is not totally to our liking.

In reality, generally speaking, the peer group that our children deal with daily has a more profound effect on them than their teacher does. However, without a doubt, a very problematic teacher can have a traumatic effect on our children and this has to be dealt with directly. Yet, dealing with a school and its administration is often a sensitive issue. We are dealing with human emotion and the delicate sphere of an individual's self-esteem. If we were in the teacher's position, would our reactions be so different? One needs to communicate appropriately and to be specific with praise whenever possible when dealing with school administration and staff.

In order to help their children, parents need to be their children's advocate in the school system. Instead of being irritated at a school or at a teacher's limitations, parents need to be proactive and see what would help their children with the available options. We can always stress the negative in a situation, but teaching children excellent coping skills is perhaps one of the best gifts we can give them. If children are resentful toward authority (mirroring their parents' responses to their school), they can end up becoming resentful toward religious authority figures in general, greatly compromising the small amount of *emunas chachamim* that exists in our generation. Parents pay a great price if they have not yet worked out their issues with authority figures.

Let it be emphasized that the above-mentioned words are not words to help promote the status quo of our schools when difficult situations exist. A parent needs to advocate change in school systems when problems are apparent. Often, choices of schools are limited for a variety of reasons, so parents need to work with their given options. In such cases, there are many areas in which we can help our children cope. We need to *daven* that we make the correct choices, that our *hishtadlus* (effort) to help our children should be sufficient, and that we should merit to see our children continue in the ways of the Torah.

6 *Teaching a child to work with criticism*

THE DEGREE OF one's level of sensitivity directly corresponds to one's sense of being criticized. Insults differ from criticism. One must learn to differentiate between the two. People may be insulting to others due to anger or jealousy, but there are cases where constructive criticism may be given from which we may all benefit.

It is true that in some situations those being critical could be more tactful, but the actual content of the suggestions might be worth listening to and one may learn from those very words. However, if only the hurt feelings are being dwelt upon, whatever might be learned from another's observations will be overshadowed by emotion and subjective reaction. Even if there is only 10 percent of the truth in the criticism, this 10 percent can be helpful for the problem at hand.

On a more philosophical level, if you were not meant to be the recipient of these comments, Hashem would not have had this occurrence take place. This does not mean that the criticism must be accepted in total, but one can accept the portion which might be useful in that particular situation. For example, you meant to help a person, but you inadvertently harmed him instead. Learning from this experience could mean that you need to be clearer in your communication to avoid misunderstandings. A person can also learn from criticism to be more cautious in confiding in certain individuals. Confidential information can sometimes be misconstrued by others and come back to you in a most unexpected fashion. There is much to be learned from one's mistakes.

When criticism directly affects one's self-esteem, different attitudes need to be stressed. When one feels that one is under attack, it is helpful to remember one's good traits. Writing these traits on a paper may seem rather simplistic, but may be quite helpful. Thus, one can feel, "Perhaps I have limitations, but I do have characteristics that are admirable."

Ultimately, if one has internalized the feeling that one has enough admirable qualities, accepting criticism becomes less of a major situation. In other words, one needs to be a big enough person to be able to take it, i.e. she has enough positive attributes to fall back on when criticism is given.

Believing in one's abilities and potential abilities is a true goal of the Torah. There are times when one may be criticized for taking a religious stance. All great leaders who have taken a stand were not loved by all. We know that Moshe Rabbeinu was criticized by *Bnei Yisrael* in the Midbar and yet he continued to do the will of Hashem. An understanding of the last line of *Megillas Esther* reflects the idea that Mordechai was loved by the majority of the people (but not the entire population), according to Rashi. Yet neither Moshe Rabbeinu nor Mordechai were deterred from doing the will of Hashem due to individuals' negative reactions. The true *"posek acharon"* (final decision) is reflected in the leaders of our generation, who are steeped in the wells of Torah. Criticism did not deter them from doing the will of Hashem.

Accustoming one's self to *mussar* can be a humbling experience, unless one becomes extremely self-effacing and is depressed by it. One needs to always build the good within in order to be able to accept criticism intelligently.

The ability to integrate constructive criticism and yet affirm one's essential self-worth is a never-ending struggle for balance towards which goal all human beings need to work.

7 Helping a child deal with his negative emotions

WHEN A CHILD seems to have difficulty in dealing with negative emotions, a parent should first try to find the cause of his child's apparent unhappiness. A child can sometimes find that his teacher appears to be distant and abrupt, or he may be angry due to a continued family feud with his siblings. The child may be having social problems or he may be worried about a situation within the family (i.e. illness or parental arguments). He may feel inept in his performance in school and would prefer to seem negative, rather than try to achieve and then fail.

A child needs to be reassured when worried, and concrete problem-solving techniques need to be applied when parents want to improve certain situations. An example might be wherein a parent works directly with siblings fighting, or works with the child's teacher on a daily basis. Concrete encouragement often speaks louder than philosophizing. A sense of negativity often reflects a sense of giving up that the child has come to accept. Low frustration tolerance may seem almost inherent in certain children.

However, when parents role-model perseverance — not giving up — it is a gift that they are giving to their child. One way of not giving up is showing an alternative method in dealing with a problematic situation, as mentioned previously. A child can be taught to either handle the circumstances differently, or envision it differently. This can be seen in a situation where a child is very frustrated when he is not able to tie his shoes and continually gives up. The parent can teach this patiently, in a variety of ways. A parent can say, "Right goes under left," or feel the actual movement of the child's fingers over and over, to learn by experience. This reflects the concrete problem-solving attitude towards tying shoelaces. Buying shoes with Velcro ties is another way of dealing with this frustrating situation. This need not be a "giving up" alternative, unless the parent envisions this as such. The parent can say: "While you have these sneakers, we'll have more time to learn how to tie the other shoes." This reflects a different way of viewing the problem. It may not be immediate, but we are working on the ultimate solution. The message is that you are not a failure, because we are not viewing it as such. Negativity is shown in how one views a situation.

Using positive reinforcement can also help change negative behavior that has become habitual. If a child constantly finds reasons to complain or teases his siblings, rewards can be given for "complaint-free" or "tease-free" days. The parent needs to find an attainable goal so as to not further frustrate the child, and should offer rewards that are meaningful to the child. These can be non-material rewards, such as time alone with parents. Experiencing success helps breed future success and helps lift the spirits of all children. By developing solutions to problems, the child begins to be more hopeful and views things in a more positive sense.

On a more general level, the parent needs to scrutinize himself and ask: "What is my reaction to daily events? How quickly do I respond negatively to frustrating circumstances?" Many incidents occur daily in one's life, and we note that what makes a difference in people's abilities and attitudes is their reaction to pain and discomfort. A parent often needs to envision situations in a more positive light as a role model, in order to imbue a sense of hope in his children. Seeing the good in a seemingly difficult situation is an example of re-envisioning a problem.

Reminding children how the family has weathered many great storms can also be meaningful. Changing children's negative attitudes takes work, both from parent and child. Yet a positive outlook on life can only be beneficial to children and to all those who touch their lives.

8 *Teaching a child compromise — problem-solving methods*

ONE OF THE most cherished life-time tools that a parent can give to his child is that of teaching the benefits and abilities of being able to compromise. We see in *Chazal: Hama'avir al middosav, mochlin al kol pesha'av* (He who forgives another's character flaws is forgiven of all his sins). To compromise in daily life occurrences is virtuous (except in the area of definitive ethical values). Being able to understand another person's needs (even if it reflects their character flaws) reflects a higher expression of *ahavas Yisrael*. This is particularly helpful for obstinate children who find it very difficult to accept any opinion but their own. Parents need to show themselves as role models when working on compromising with family members (especially for children who seem to be very set in their ways).

Teaching how to compromise effectively is also teaching children how to avoid power struggles with other human beings (besides their parents). In this way, both parties involved can maintain their dignity and feel that their opinions are being validated to some degree. Neither side may receive totally what they desire, but each one's self-respect is maintained.

To initially problem-solve, one needs to attempt to be non-judgmental and be open to new suggestions that were not "on their agenda." Each person needs to either verbalize or write down his own issue, and the place where he is stuck. Then, each side writes down possible solutions to this challenging situation. One needs to listen respectfully to each solution suggested (not showing anger at unworkable suggestions), and then together problem-solve possible solutions. When a person's ideas are written on paper, he feels only the more validated and less resentful when the final outcome is decided. A parent can actually create a written contract with both parties' signatures, if the issues involved are of a serious nature. This technique is most helpful with teenagers, as well as strong-willed children.

Teaching appreciation to your child — dugmah chayah — being a role model 9

SO MUCH OF a person's responses to life are connected to what his individual expectations are, in relation to every given situation. If one expects that marriage will be an answer to all of a person's problems, he undoubtedly will be disappointed. The same personality limitations that all humans possess will exist, with or without a spouse. Having a caring person to share life with is a great *brachah*, but what are you expecting this person to do, to change the scope of your universe? If one expects marriage to be as it is portrayed in the world of drama and media, one can never truly appreciate the daily reality of living with a spouse.

And it is with reality that many individuals encounter experience after experience — disappointed that this wasn't the job that you had hoped for, or the relationship that you had hoped for. When a person speaks of realistic expectations, realistic can be idealistic if one tempers one's expectations.

Truly being *sameach b'chelko* is appreciating life from moment to moment. Having *bitachon* that "*gam zu l'tovah*," this too is for the good, decreases anxiety in relation to daily frustrating occurrences. So often what we worry about for days never occurs, and what we would never dream about occurs instead. A person has lower expectations if he has *hakaras hatov* for life's small blessings. One will not put all his energy and hope in the vacation he hopes to have for two weeks out of the year, if he appreciates the time that he spent playing Frisbee with his children, unexpectedly, one afternoon. That spontaneous hour can be remembered more lovingly by the family than the two-week vacation that had daily rain (or daily family fighting).

A parent needs to verbally frame life's experiences with appreciation when speaking to his children, acknowledging *Hashgachah Pratis* and the wonders of all that we see around us. This appreciation creates a most satisfied and happy human being. Such a person can laugh if something goes wrong and quickly attempt to find a solution (because, to begin with, he didn't expect everything to always go perfectly). Parents need to be role models for the child, seeing the good in what appears to be deficient in the present moment.

Harchavas hada'as (clarity of perception) can occur from undisturbed thoughts and the ability to focus on the task at hand. If one continually focuses on life's limitations and not life's potentials, one then lacks this clarity of vision, as feelings of sadness can become all-consuming. Through true *hakaras hatov* of Hashem we can see through the *aspaklaria hame'irah* (the clear window of vision), and be able to use more of our own actual individual potential on a daily basis.

Helping children with socialization skills 10

THOUGH THE LACK of socialization skills in certain children is truly a learning disability, it is something that can be worked with, to some degree, at home. The optimal method for learning socialization skills is through a group, but this format is not always available or desirable, depending on the individual child's temperament. A child might be uncomfortable in a group setting (as well as a child's parent), and instead need to focus on the acquisition of these skills on a one-to-one basis.

There are socialization-skills books, which have pictures of given social situations and captions suggesting children's appropriate responses to these situations. Though often used with speech therapists and special-education tutors, parents can sometimes use such materials if they are not didactic, but playful in their approach to it. One page might show how a child opens a conversation, or how a child asserts himself appropriately. A parent can ask questions about the picture and use humor in describing the situation. Since the children in the picture do not appear to look like the child's friends or family members, this method is usually not so threatening or uncomfortable to children. The questions one asks his children need to have answers, and a parent has to be prepared to offer solutions for these complicated social situations. The conversations need to be more philosophical and general, not focusing on the child's particular issues (unless the child brings it up and wants to talk about it). A parent needs to be non-judgmental in this discussion in order to elicit a sense of comfort and a more open response from his child.

A more creative parent can role-play social situations and show possible appropriate social responses to difficult situations. A parent can show what spatially appropriate distance feels like to another person (if a child has that issue), again using humor rather than appearing to be condescending. If a parent himself has an issue in certain social situations, he can tell his child how he functions in that situation — i.e. feeling shy in a given situation. Seeing how an adult may have a similar struggle can normalize the child's feelings about this challenge, and give him more fortitude in which to overcome this issue in his life.

Clearly, not every parent feels comfortable in assuming

the role of a social-skills trainer to his children, and professional help in this area can be very beneficial. Some children do not pick up social skills naturally, and need to be taught to look for other people's reactions to their words and actions. Positive reinforcement for good eye contact and good conversational ability can always be given to children to help build self-esteem and reinforce positive change.

Helping the child who is teased — ## 11
scapegoat of the classroom

CERTAIN TYPES OF children (and adults) seem to more easily become the scapegoat in given social situations. Their lack of self-confidence is somehow sensed by others, and they feel that it is safe to antagonize such a non-threatening person. Thus, certain people become targets due to their apparent vulnerability.

A person can become a scapegoat due to being neglected or overly indulged as a child. Being neglected obviously causes children to doubt their abilities. As so little attention is being given to them, their sense of self has not been strongly defined. Such lack of self-confidence can be sensed by others. Overly pampered children are also unaware of their capabilities as they have rarely been give the chance to use their potential. Thus, such children only feel secure when protective adults are with them (whether it is their parents or other adults paralleling this role).

It is crucial to analyze a parent's behavior towards his child. A parent needs to ask himself: "Am I giving my child opportunities to display her abilities and talents, or is she sometimes getting lost in the daily activities of life? Or am I so fearful that my child will experience a sense of failure that I hesitate to allow her to experiment with new activities?" Either possibility needs to be considered.

Besides working on these crucial attitudes that help to create scapegoats, there are concrete steps that you can presently take in order to help your child. Speaking to your child's teachers can be of utmost importance. A teacher can improve your child's image in class by stressing her talents or putting her in leadership positions (that she is able to manage). A parent can request that his child join a classmate (a classmate that might be an appropriate friend for the child) in a class project. If a child is too shy, an external structure, such as a class project, may help her to learn to more appropriately socialize with classmates. A parent might suggest to a child to invite one or two of the least non-friendly classmates with her on a Sunday outing, in order to show her that she can be liked by others.

A parent needs to attempt to look at his child objectively and see if there are any extremely inappropriate modes of behavior that the child exhibits towards others. This could be immature mannerisms or a slovenly appearance, or any type of self-expression that is negative.

Through positive reinforcement, behavior can be modified. Star charts can be created and much praise can be given to a child who is attempting to improve herself. Telling children that you want them to be the best that they can be is a more positive way to approach this subject, rather than, "I've had enough of this behavior."

A child needs to learn how to respond to cruel comments, as they are given at various times throughout a person's lifetime. Teaching to ignore or putting thoughts in your mind while they are saying it to anesthetize the pain are common responses to this problem. At times, sarcastic remarks in return are an appropriate way to quiet a bothersome classmate, but this response needs to be carefully measured to ascertain its effectiveness. (This can sometimes escalate arguments.) Learning to agree with the teaser is a very helpful response, but needs to be practiced in order to be effective. (An example of this might be a response to someone being called "Four-eyes." A child can then respond to this teasing by stating: "I'm happy you like my new glasses." By agreeing with the teaser, there is little place for the teaser to go.)

A parent can play an important role by providing comfort, by empathizing with the actual teasing. Sharing the fact that others may have hurt you or your spouse's feelings sometime in your own lives gives your child a sense of being less alone, which is helpful in itself.

At times therapy may be helpful if this problem is severe. Families often unknowingly create negative patterns and roles for its members. Thus, a family sometimes needs to create more positive roles for its members, in order for people to change their sense of self in a more global way. A scapegoated child desiring change needs to feel more successful in all areas of life — especially that of the family unit.

In general, working on a child's self-esteem is the most essential ingredient for success in working with the problem of scapegoating. If self-esteem is increased, a child will feel less vulnerable to others and less reliant upon others' continual acceptance of them. The teaser will surely find her cruel entertainment in another arena!

12 Humility and self-promotion — a delicate balance

THOUGH WE SPEAK of the greatness of humility, and of having a "*ruach nemochah*," the reality of our 21st-century world seems to scream the opposite message. There are only a certain amount of schools, a certain amount of "good" *shidduchim* available — the competition seems to be so great. We cannot ask *mechanchim* to open up more schools just because it is our desire. It is a tremendous undertaking to hire staff, to pay them, hope that parents pay tuition, hope that the pipes don't break, etc. We can complain about our educational systems, but to actually attempt to create a school ourselves is an enormous undertaking. Thus, the amount of schools that are available is limited.

In general, our resources are limited, and self-promotion is sometimes an avenue that we all need to take. Yet how do we preserve our *anivus*, our humility, which is our spiritual dignity, in such a competitive world? Getting your child a job in a sleep-away camp can take as much effort as getting a child into a school. A girl's self-worth can unfortunately be weighed by the part that she receives in her school play.

One can speak to a mother who is totally exasperated after speaking to *shadchanim* about her daughter, feeling more like a salesman than a parent. A parent has to be sure that she is in a calm state of mind when she embarks upon such a call, to ensure that the *shadchan's* vision of her is exemplary.

A person can get caught up in a "*kochi v'otzem yadi*" mentality (I caused all this myself by my actions), missing the point of appropriate *hishtadlus*. It is true that sometimes it is very necessary to remind a person that your child exists and is very worthwhile, but there can be a thin line between being appropriately assertive and being irritating. In one community, it might be more socially appropriate to be a "nag," and in another it is considered undignified (i.e. "Who wants to deal with a family like this?" — one might ask.)

One needs to remind oneself who is truly the *Baʹal Habayis* of this world — perhaps by saying a *kapitel* of *Tehillim*, or giving *tzedakah* — before making such difficult phone calls. It is written in the *hakdamah* of *Shaʹar Habitachon* in *Chovos Halevavos* that if a person puts his trust in something or someone else, rather than Hashem, the actual providence is given over to that person or thing (i.e. as with the stock market). One needs to clarify his reality in order to maintain this delicate balance. Thus, it is not just a person's way of speech that shows *bitachon*, but in the way that they strive to think in such difficult situations.

On a practical level, when one differentiates between assertiveness and aggressiveness, the difference is subtle. If one states feelings without anger, and states consequences of actions, one is appropriately assertive. When statements become filled with anger, the assertiveness becomes aggressiveness. Being quietly persistent, yet being aware of other people's boundaries and comfort level, is again appropriate. If one goes past these boundaries and becomes aggressive, one creates mistrust and the opposite of one's desired results.

When a person over-identifies with the need to be "self-promoting," he needs to be aware that if Hashem does not desire this end result, no action can cause it to occur. We can see this idea when Yehoshua came to conquer Yericho. Yehoshua saw that the wall was strong and that it was impenetrable. Within the laws of nature he could not be victorious. His *hishtadlus* was to promise to take the spoils of Yericho and dedicate them to the Beis Hamikdash. He would give the spoils to Hashem, rather than to the people with him. This action caused the wall to crumble, which began the process of conquering Eretz Yisrael. This is an example of the delicate balance that exists between *hishtadlus* and *bitachon*, and we need to *daven* for *siyatta diShmaya* in order to take appropriate action in any given situation.

SELF-ESTEEM ISSUES

Improving your child's self-esteem in a real way 13

COMPLIMENTING A CHILD is very important for a parent to do, but it is perhaps only believable when this compliment is very specific. In order for a child to better see his positive attributes, a general process already needs to have been developed, in which this compliment reflects these building blocks of self-esteem.

The first step in building a child's self-esteem is to allow the child self-acceptance. Do we as parents permit our child to have feelings and thoughts that we dislike, or do we invalidate them immediately? Do we honestly accept him as he presently stands or do we incessantly push our expectations on him? Our negotiation of our child's ideas does not cause them to disappear. This child will merely bury these "unacceptable" feelings, not knowing how to deal with them. On the other hand, when we accept our child's feelings as valid, our child will come to accept and appreciate himself as a worthwhile human being. Instead of being overly self-critical, the child will learn that his feelings are worth being shared and discussed.

Another obvious impediment to self-confidence is name-calling, which parents may engage in when they are on the brink of frustration. Though most parents do not feel that their behavior is desirable, they do not know alternative ways of reacting. One needs to try and initiate new forms of communication skills with one's children to prevent outbursts (which is another topic of discussion in itself). By acquiring new ways of reacting to children one helps to produce a more self-confident child.

Positive reinforcement of desirable actions is a technique used by many parents to encourage their child to choose "good" rather than "bad" behavior. While this method can be quite successful, it must be used with caution. When one child alone is rewarded, other siblings may resent this special treatment and harbor jealousy and anger toward this sibling. In addition, the child may learn to identify himself as the most unruly and misbehaving sibling in the family. He may wonder why he is the only one in the family who's being singled out for the behavior-modification plan. In order for a child to feel self-esteem he needs to perceive that he is equal to his siblings and is an integral part of the family.

Leveling is a crucial step in building a child's self-confidence. Children need to feel at least equal to their siblings before feeling positive feelings about themselves. Let us consider the use of leveling in responding to problematic behavior. When a child has a temper tantrum, for example, how should we react? Giving immediate attention will only cause the child to repeat the tantrums. Ignoring the child will not be useful, since the need for attention will remain unsatisfied. A child needs to be shown, "we accept your need for attention, but we are a unit and work for common goals." This message can be conveyed by giving the child a lot of attention, not at the moment that she demands it, but when she is involved in social activities such as working with siblings in clean-up, or doing homework. Thus, the child will receive attention and also have a sense of herself as being part of a group effort — thus removing the stigma of being the "problem child."

Until now, emphasis has been on what not to do, and how to help a child feel part of a group successfully. Yet how do we show children that they are unique and special individuals? One way is to establish a time when one or both parents spend time alone with their children. This time should be non-pressured and fun in its nature. The time spent together should convey to the child that he is considered charming, loveable, and fun to be with, which will help him to develop a high opinion of himself.

A child's self-respect will grow further if parents encourage the development of a personal talent in which the child can feel pride. This special ability may be in sports, music or any skill imaginable. If parents find it difficult to find such a point, they can help him to create one. For example, a child can be encouraged to excel in kindness — the gift of giving. Parents can show enthusiasm when a child helps a neighbor, tutors a child, or assists a person who is ailing. (Such work may be done at no charge or minimal wage.) Besides being a good deed, learning to help others brings great self-satisfaction and the child will come to be seen as a giving, caring human being.

The above-mentioned methods can be used for all children, since all can benefit from an increase in self-confidence. However, if these steps do not produce substantial change and a child's problem seems more complex, professional help should be sought. Other issues may be involved, making it difficult for children to increase their self-confidence.

After surveying different methods to help a child acquire

a sense of self-worth, we see that a great deal depends on parents' active involvement. One cannot expect positive change unless new modes of behavior and attitudes are implemented, all very well worth the outcome of a more self-confident, happy child.

14 Helping your child feel competent at home — breaks, working towards goals

PERHAPS THE MAIN difference between an overly stressful and not so stressful Erev Pesach is related to one's family. If a person envisions a time period as "manageable," one can organize one's mind and thoughts more clearly. Organization, positive reinforcement, and breaks are the key to a more manageable Erev Pesach.

A most important message that a parent can convey to his child is a sense of that child's competency. One can feel warmth and love from one's family, but not feel self-confidence in one's actual abilities. Saying to a child, "I know that you can do it," is a limited message of belief in a child, and is only a beginning in helping to actualize a child's potential abilities. By actively involving a child in tasks that involve some degree of responsibility, a child's true ability can be experienced most directly. In this way, involving one's children in Pesach preparations can be a very constructive project, helping to build their sense of competency. Though many women prefer cleaning women and babysitters Erev Pesach (if financially feasible), the experience of creating a "battlefield project" with one's children can help create unity and single purposefulness among siblings.

If one embarks (approximately 4-6 weeks before Pesach) upon writing a "battle plan" for preparations for Pesach, and involves one's children in its creation, the children's participation and investment will be increased greatly. Discussions need to take place regarding which rooms will be done when and which children are capable of which jobs, and then decisions need to be made. Actual dates and commitments of time and responsibility need to be determined. Children of most ages are capable of contributing, be it polishing silver or lining shelves — some jobs need not be done perfectly. If working, children then feel more involved and constructive and do not look at themselves as an impediment to Pesach cleaning.

Another category of more "interesting" chores are those such as clothes-buying and goods-buying. Such work needs to be inserted into a more tedious-sounding schedule, in order to insure variety (and sanity) in the weeks before Pesach. Perhaps one child prefers a "foot outing," another to buy tablecloths and utensils. Each child can go out with a parent to do some type of more "interesting" chore in the days before Pesach.

In relation to positive reinforcement, small rewards for work can be offered on Erev Pesach, be it through special privileges, more desirable Pesach work, or other rewards. These rewards raise the morale of one's children, and reinforce their general cooperative, working behavior. I know of a mother who spends comparatively little for *akifomen* presents, but instead allows every child to choose a twenty-dollar present to buy before Pesach. This present is received after all pre-Pesach chores are completed, and gives the children a sense of pride in their work.

The third category that helps pre-Pesach stress is that of creating breaks. Breaks are blocks of time before Pesach which help create a mental distraction for one's family. Though this idea may seem ludicrous when one envisions the time before Pesach, if one thinks of the tremendous mental and physical strain that is often removed after any type of a short vacation of "mental rest," this can also be applied to Pesach. This distraction can be two hours in the park, a visit to a pizza store, a *bikur cholim* visit, or any activity which is somewhat meaningful or pleasurable (which is not connected to Pesach). The corporate world has found that coffee breaks improve the general performance of its staff, and this also holds true with a family's work performance.

In relation to breaks, another type of break (though seemingly simple) needs to be reiterated. If a child seems to strongly desire a parent's attention, it is often more worthwhile to spend five or ten minutes and stop one's pre-Pesach schedule to redirect a child's play and sibling interaction. In general, wherever possible, one should make a point of talking to one's children as a parent works, to help them feel that they are not forgotten and that they are an essential part of the family.

Though Erev Pesach is often stressful, the degree of stress does not have to be overwhelming. One can help to instill good *middos* in one's children during this time period by teaching them responsibility, showing by example how to praise when praise is due, and modeling *bitachon* by showing them that one can take a break (to preserve one's health)! In this way, one can truly go beyond one's boundaries, and simultaneously help the emotional and spiritual growth of one's children.

Verbal praise 15

VERBAL PRAISE OF all family members actually raises the potential of each individual. One cannot underestimate the value of verbal praise to one's family members, especially on a daily basis. The power of *dibbur* actually affects a person's potential in a positive way.

According to Chabad *Chassidus*, one needs to continually give words of praise to fellow Jews, in order to awaken the actual good within them. This idea can be understood when we look at *Parashas Emor*. *Emor* means "to say" — in grammar, it has the form of present tense and command tense. As if to say, whatever it is that *Emor* is teaching us, and the word Torah is from the expression to teach, the utterance is a constant one and a desirable one. The teaching is that by saying positive, uplifting words, the words themselves carry the power of bringing out the positive aspects of a person and help him overcome any negative traits. Then by constantly uttering the positive, the negative will be less and less until it eventually disappears. By stressing the good, the negative elements eventually dissipate, as one's identity becomes a positive and constructive one.

We also see in Rambam's *Hilchos Talmud Torah* that a *talmid chacham* is only permitted to look at the good in a person while he is speaking to him. Reb Nachman of Breslov also expresses this idea in *Lekutei Maharan*, where he speaks of the idea of "*V'hisbonanta al mekomo v'einenu*" — "If one meditates about the place (of the evil person), he will no longer exist" (*Tehillim*, 37).

If one will truly contemplate the good points of a fellow Jew (even if generally he may be viewed as appearing evil), we will see that he has many *mitzvos* to his credit and deserves to be given the benefit of the doubt and to be considered in a positive light. We are actually assisting him to improve himself, as our positive vision and words to describe the person are elevating his potential. Thus, in a similar vein, by our looking at the unique and special goodness of each family member, we can assist in their spiritual development.

Certain parents may find it difficult to continually praise their children, as they may have received a more European upbringing, stressing what is missing in each child. "Where's the two points on this test to make it 100 percent?" is a statement that many of us may have been accustomed to hearing. Yet this generation finds such messages generally unhelpful; they make a child feel "never good enough." We need to realize that our children can easily receive praise and encouragement from the secular society around them, which continually stresses positive vibes and feeling good. Our children need to find this sense of feeling good in our own homes and schools, and not look elsewhere for such a need. Due to great competition in our society — be it in relation to *shidduchim* or acceptance into certain yeshivos — a person can easily feel dejected and second-class in different circumstances. Thus, it is even more essential to verbalize praise, to help children re-evaluate themselves in a positive manner, and envision a hopeful future for them.

16 *Difficulty in hearing praises — children with low self-esteem?*

PARENTS OFTEN COMPLAIN of children who have difficulty in hearing praise and who seem to actually become irritated. These children feel that the praise is unnecessary or insincere. What can a parent do in such a circumstance, when he wants to compliment such a child?

Initially, one needs to analyze why this child finds it difficult to accept praise. Is his self-esteem weak, and he feels that any type of praise is flattery? Parents need to analyze how they are expressing their positive sentiments towards their children, and how they are being received.

If a parent is very specific in his praise to his child, there is less of a possibility that the sincerity of the parent's words will be challenged. If a parent says: "When you ran to give the chair to Shlomo, you made him feel like a million dollars," the child can feel the sincerity of these words, as his actual actions are being recaptured. This helps to validate the actual compliment. If we would say instead, "You're such a good boy," these words might have less of an effect on a child, as the phrase is too general.

Parents' praise has to also reflect the parents' actual value system, and what the child knows is truly important to them. If a parent doesn't value getting 100 percent on tests, getting excited about such a mark on a spelling test means little to children. They know intrinsically that these words are more "lip service," rather than heart-felt expressions. Fathers can compliment new clothing, and not have bought a new suit for years.

This is not to say that one should never compliment something that is not of important value to oneself. Sharing excitement and enthusiasm with a child can be a form of *chessed*. However, it is not the most effective way of building a child's self-esteem, as he may sense that you care little about the subject at hand.

17 *Children misbehaving after being complimented*

How should a parent respond when a child misbehaves after being complimented? Does the misbehavior cancel out the compliment? Again, would we like to lose a bonus that we received at work because we happened to come to work late for two days in a row? We can understand being docked from work because we are late, but losing the bonus that we acquired for hard work seems to be a very unfair consequence. Thus, as parents, we have to refrain from saying statements such as, "I thought you were a good boy. I guess that I was wrong." The compliment for good behavior is well deserved. It doesn't deserve to be taken away. A better response to such a situation would be: "I know that you're good — you're trying to fool me," or "You think I'm so silly that I believe that this is really who you are!" A parent can also say: "A 'Schwartz' (the child's family name) doesn't behave this way. I'm really confused."

Clearly, this is not the only possible response to a child's misbehavior. Yet, the initial belief in the child is necessary to make the turn-around in behavior that much easier. "If I am actually a 'good' child, then WHAT is going on here?" thinks the child. The transformation is that of someone coming back to who they really are.

After this initial verbal reframing of the negative situation, a parent does need to give a consequence when necessary. The type of consequence needed depends on the actual misbehavior involved, as a child needs to see that there is a consequence to negative behavior. However, a parent has to truly believe in his child's ability to mend his ways, and not verbalize: "It's okay. I know that you'll do it ten times again." A child picks up on a parent's true feelings, and then does not believe in his own ability to change. Thus, we need to believe in the special abilities of every Jewish *neshamah*, which is an actual part of Hashem (even our children)!

CHILDREN — SPECIFIC BEHAVIORAL CHALLENGES

Different ways to deal with temper tantrums 18

TEMPER TANTRUMS CAN be frightening to families, especially when those tantrums continue on an ongoing basis. It can be frightening to the child who feels that he is losing control. The anxiety it generates can be felt for a prolonged period of time, long after the outburst itself. A child's unbridled anger causes parents to feel helpless, and a parent may begin to question himself and wonder who is really in control in the house. And yet, for both adults and children alike, no one feels comfortable with uncontrollable negative emotions.

A child chooses this behavior as a way to vent feelings for a variety of reasons. The most common and simple cause of milder temper tantrums is that of a child who is spoiled. Such a child will often have his parents wrapped around his finger. He will know how to manipulate his parents and will understand that his parents' embarrassment over a screaming child will cause them to give in to anything rather than hear their child screaming in public. A parent needs to scrutinize his reactions to his child's behavior which allow for such behavior to exist publicly.

To change a child's reaction, a parent needs to change his initial response to his child. If a child really believes that "no" is "no" and not "maybe," perhaps these tantrums will not occur. If a child really believes that screaming publicly will only incur worse consequences later on, perhaps a child will attempt other means to gain what he desires. A parent must honestly take stock and ask himself if he is being consistent in his words and actions with his child. If one is consistent, tantrums are less likely to occur, because the child knows that the tantrum will not change things, and the child will also know that there will be negative consequences.

A more serious type of temper tantrum is that of the very frustrated child. This is the child that gets into a fight with siblings and begins to have a temper tantrum when she is unable to express herself verbally. She is unable to express herself and deal with anger, which causes her to become more and more frustrated until her emotions can only be expressed through tears and general uncontrollability. This type of child cannot usually be reached by a rational problem-solving parent, as the child's response itself is no longer logical. Consumed by a feeling of "not being understood," a parent's logical explanation of the child's problem will not dissipate the pain. Instead, a child needs to have an illogical response, in a sense. As the child cannot find the words to express her outrage, a parent can try and formulate what he thinks the child might be feeling. An example of this might be: "Chani started up with you. She called you stupid — it's not fair."

Though Chani may not appreciate her parent taking her sister's side, this is often necessary to help enable the child to form her thoughts and give them passageway to leave the realm of hysteria. Once the screaming child is calmer, a more honest appraisal of the situation can be made by both siblings.

In such a situation, punishment for the tantrum is not

usually helpful. The child's anger was due to extreme frustration, and not due to a desire to manipulate others. After such an episode, attempting prevention of future outbursts is a more constructive way of dealing with this problem.

Prevention of tantrums could involve discussing ways of appropriately expressing anger. Asking a child what she might have wanted her parent to do in the actual situation is another example of what can be done. However, the child's suggestion may not be able to be carried out in a future circumstance, and a parent needs to explain why this idea would not be possible. Ultimately, a child needs to be allowed to express frustration and see her parent's desire to work together with her.

At times, a child can feel very justified in his extreme anger and find it difficult to let go. Perhaps at times the analogy of Shimon and Levi can be mentioned. Though Shimon and Levi felt justified in their vengeance towards the city of Shechem, according to classic commentators, Yaakov felt that this action was not the best way to respond to the heinous crime done to Dina. One needs to use anger, but directed towards the ultimate goal of being *mikadesh shem Shamayim*, and not the opposite.

Sometimes temper tantrums reflect a more global problem that is occurring in the home among family members. It might be a family, medical or even an emotional crisis. Whatever the cause, a child can sometimes almost absorb the tension of the house, internalizing an overwhelming feeling of tension, and is only able to vent these feelings in fits of rage. Such anger expresses the anxiety of the home and the problem needs to be resolved within the family system.

In some cases, uncontrollable tantrums reflect a more

severe problem within an individual child and professional help is necessary. In such cases, a more in-depth approach needs to be followed.

Working with anger is a lifetime task that is difficult for adults and children. Yet, helping a child effectively cope with negative emotions is a tremendous tool that all parents can give to their children.

19 Sibling rivalry

WE CAN SEE from *Bereishis* that sibling rivalry is inherent among human beings. Kayin and Hevel could not live together on the same earth, and we also encounter similar situations with Yosef and his brothers. In fact, our first *galus* to Mitzrayim was due to the problems between Yosef and his brothers. Each side, however, felt that they were acting *l'shem Shamayim*. Yosef felt that his father needed to know about his brothers' actions, which seemed totally unacceptable in Yosef's eyes, according to the Torah's principles. His brothers saw reasons to believe that Yosef was *chayav misah* — Yosef had acted in a manner deserving the death penalty. Therefore, throwing Yosef into the snake-filled pit seemed justified to his brothers. The actual beginning of dissension among the brothers seemed to result from Yosef's having been given the multi-colored coat by his father. Though everything occurs because of Divine Providence, there is much that can be learned and applied from these sources when we are working with our own children.

People have a tendency to compare themselves to those who are nearest to them: neighbors, co-workers, siblings, etc. Sometimes, there is a feeling of jealousy if a person doesn't sense a comfortable place for himself in this world. If children or adults feel secure in their sense of self-worth and their abilities, they may feel a minimal amount of jealousy. If a child can say, "This is what my mother likes about me," then there is less of a chance for intense sibling rivalry.

In general, children need to learn to express their feelings in words — not with physical force or name-calling. It is of utmost importance for the parent to teach the child that it is understandable if she gets angry, but that the reason for anger should be voiced. In working toward the resolution, the child should understand that although she feels justified, the other person's side must also be heard. Children's fighting is a natural avenue for teaching problem-solving techniques.

However, if the children are too angry to try to negotiate peacefully, a parent can model the area of negotiation and help the two sides to become reconciled. In such a situation the goal is to eventually teach children to negotiate without adult intervention — a technique they will find quite useful for many years in the future. If actual physical fighting does occur, children should be separated into different rooms. Once they are apart in other rooms, they are more easily calmed down and communication, as well as negotiation, is more possible.

If a child emerges victimized in most of the crises, the parent needs to scrutinize how the child's position in the family can be improved. If this child is viewed by the siblings as being incompetent, the parents should then stress where she has been competent. By showing the hurt child that she need not feel like a victim, the role of the child in the family can be changed for the better. Such children are often less demanding, and therefore parents need to make a specific time to speak to this child and show that their thoughts are of her (i.e. "I bought this fruit for you because I know you like it"). By increasing her self-importance, she can emerge stronger in sibling confrontations. At such times, giving children joint projects can also be helpful, so that they can learn to work together naturally. A parent might remind the sister to buy a birthday present for her brother as well. This tends to enhance children's sense of family unity.

Some children "*chepper*" due to boredom, as play-fighting leads to real fighting. Activities should be structured more diligently for children. There are also times when children have difficult days at school and they let it out on anyone around the house. Sensing a child's initial agitation upon coming home from school can serve as a warning sign to the parent and the situation can be handled accordingly. Whether offering the child some pleasant distraction or by listening to the child's school woes, the parent might lessen the child's unhappiness and possibly prevent sibling fighting.

It is true that "battling siblings" may become very close in their adult years. However, helping them to be closer in their younger years also will only add strength to their existing relationship. There will be fewer unresolved issues that recur between brother and sister if problem-solving techniques and clarity are utilized in the earlier years. Any efforts attempted in this area will be greatly appreciated by the children who will, hopefully, live together many years, and will as a result have many pleasant moments to remember.

The impulsive child — redirecting your child on the "fast lane of the highway" 20

CERTAIN CHILDREN SEEM to feel a certain excitement when breaking rules, and find enjoyment in continually changing the structure in the daily schedule that you are attempting to create. There is a reason why Curious George is everyone's favorite character — he can always be impulsive and get into trouble, but in the end, he is the hero, and everyone loves him. In our daily lives, such impulsive behavior is generally not tolerated.

Such children often have the need to be recognized, and want to be in the center-stage of life. This is often seen in relation to males. We hear the term "male ego," which reflects the need that some men possess to be recognized and feel important in the society-at-large. Harav Samson Raphael Hirsch *zt"l* explains that men may feel innately insecure, as they know that they live "*me'afar l'eifer*" (from dust to ashes). Their existence is a physical one, and they need to constantly prove that they are something. Women generally have less of such a need, as they know they were created from a spiritual being — from the rib of Adam after he had been given a *neshamah*. Thus, they do not have such a need to prove themselves.

However, if a child has a need to be recognized by others, whether the child is a male or female, a parent or teacher cannot ignore it. The wise teacher has specific board monitors and *chazzanim* to help him (and them), and this idea can be replicated in the home. An impulsive child appreciates the adrenaline rush experienced in his impulsivity, and this needs to be replicated on a smaller level, through a positive-reinforcement system. One can see this idea when smokers attempt to quit smoking. Some use nicotine patches to help them wean themselves away from their addiction, as their bodies are so accustomed to the sensation of nicotine in their bodies. Once a type of need has been established (either positive or negative), one needs to work with this given reality.

Most impulsive children do desire to please their parents (at least at a young age), and will be willing to participate in some form of positive reinforcement that will have some redeemable payoff for them. Though it will clearly not be as exciting as previous activities, the payoff of some type of desired reward, and parent satisfaction, can be very gratifying to a child.

An impulsive child needs to see consequences of his actions spelled out for him by his parents. Though nothing may seem to faze the child, he still needs to hear the words with definite eye contact from a parent. Knowledge of this information will not necessarily change future behavior (as adrenaline rush is a powerful thing), but *chinuch* is the art of imparting knowledge and attempting to find vessels in which it can be received. This can be achieved by "ethical" story-telling, or acting out the problematic behavior that just occurred, in a dramatic manner.

Certain impulsive children have poor social skills and need cues from adults to help them realize how they affect the environment around them very directly. Role-playing appropriate eye contact helps the impulsive child better focus on appropriate behavior and responsiveness to others. Belief in the child and the child's ultimate ability to exhibit self-control is one of the most precious self-esteem builders that a parent can give to a child.

The angry child 21

THE ISSUE OF anger is one of the most difficult issues that human beings face daily. If a parent helps to work on this issue when a child is young, it is an eternal lesson that one can bestow upon a child. The ability to learn positive coping mechanisms — learning how to deal with whatever comes by without hysterical responses — is a basis for optimal mental health.

A parent needs to put emphasis upon prevention, and see what upsets his child initially. One child can be disturbed by someone playing with his toys, while another is disturbed greatly by being teased. A parent needs to choose a calm moment — the "sandbox" or "Lego" time, when the child is in a more neutral mood. When a child is in a more elated mood, he does not want to be reminded of his shortcomings and what made him upset. When he is in an angry mood, he surely does not want to be reminded of his limitations.

During this calm time, a parent needs to use cognitive restructuring — looking at the same incident in another, more positive way — in order to teach the child how to deal with the many disappointments in life. If the purpose of our lives is *tikkun hamiddos*, we need to be *dan l'chaf zechus* — stress the idea of giving the benefit of the doubt — as a way to avoid anger, and cognitively reconstruct the initially seemingly painful situation. We are teaching the child to say to himself: "I will check out what I felt, and envision another way to respond to this."

Part of a person's anger is related to a person's feeling targeted for suffering. "Why me?" is often spoken with anger and resentment. A person needs to be reminded of the *hakdamah* of *Mesilas Yesharim:* "There is not one person in one thousand who doesn't suffer afflictions. If there is this one person, he knows someone very close to him who is suffering."

Very often in life we find ourselves in situations that seem unfair. Our children need to see that we handle things in a resourceful, positive way in such circumstances, and that we avoid responding in angry ways. It is sometimes helpful to actually verbalize this, as children don't always pick up these concepts naturally. An example of this might be: "Can you imagine that I didn't receive a wedding invitation from a friend that I know for over thirty years? But I decided not to be angry until I checked into it more. It wasn't worth unnecessary aggravation. There's probably something missing here that I don't know." Or a person could verbalize: "I had to wait at the doctor for over two hours. I thought that I was going to go out of my mind. But it was actually *gam zu l'tovah*, because I had an informative conversation with Mrs. Schwartz about Nechami's school."

In relation to prevention, a child sometimes needs to be reminded in advance of situations that could cause her anger and disappointment. If a child has difficulty going to a toy store and not buying all that she sees, a parent needs to discuss this issue in advance. Using the "cushion method" discussed previously, in a neutral mood, this idea can be discussed. A parent can say: "I know how much you enjoy going to the toy store, but when you cry bitterly, it makes everyone so sad. So I really have doubts of what I should do." In this way, the parent cushions the rebuke that he is giving to his child, and the issue of the child's anger is dealt with appropriately.

Sometimes, a parent cannot avoid conflict with a child, and a child needs to know that "no" is clearly "no," and not "maybe." On the other hand, in rare circumstances, it is not worth confronting a child, if certain issues are too intense and cause too much unnecessary conflict. When a parent forces her will upon a child too often, a child may become manipulative, as well.

Parents who change their minds because their children scream long enough also become victims of their children's manipulation. Children can take advantage of their parents' indecisiveness, to achieve the results that they desire. A parent has to envision the long haul of parenting and where this "giving in" to problematic behavior will lead to.

Other areas of prevention in relation to angry children involve problem-solving the issue of anger with one's child. A parent can ask (after the fact, of course): "Why did you scream? What can we do to avoid it in the future?" If this process is done in a thorough manner, there is less of a chance that it will occur to the same degree in the future.

What techniques are available to avoid these angry outbursts? A parent can write a list of punishments and rewards in response to non-angry behavior. The punishments (consequences of action, actually) should involve something that a child would miss now, but not remember twenty years from now. Sometimes parents punish themselves if the punishment given is too severe — if an angry child is in the house all day, which one of them is truly being punished — the parent or the child?

A parent can work on improving communication with her child. Some children have complained that their parents never really listened to them, and that they had to scream out of frustration to get any real response from their parents. A parent can say: "I guess sometimes you feel so frustrated, that you can't find the words to express it. I felt so bad when you were so sad. We have to find ways — you and me — special ways to tell me what you're feeling, before you get so upset."

What are some ways to remind one's child when his negative mood begins to escalate? Sometimes using an agreed-upon password with one's child can be a helpful tool to calm down an escalating angry mood. A parent can say: "I know that sometimes you get upset and you forget your decision not to get angry. Maybe next time you start to get upset, I'll give you this special password. When you'll hear this password, it will remind you of this idea, and you'll stop. Maybe I'll say, 'Miriam, I'm on your side'…What else could I say that might be able to help?" A parent can ensure that the words will not cause embarrassment to the child by asking the child in advance.

A parent can reward the child with special stickers and rewards each time she says what she feels instead of screaming and crying. (This method needs to be created carefully, as a child may take advantage of this method.) Verbalizing negative emotion is helpful, as one can work to solve a problem easier this way rather than trying to contain problematic behavior.

There are times that a person has a right to be angry, as we see with Yaakov and the people of Shechem. Feelings of disappointment are real, and a child sometimes needs to accept these feelings of anger, and not constantly push them away. A parent can empathize with these emotions and validate them, particularly when they reflect higher principles that parents desire to stress (i.e. anger at children cheating on tests).

A parent can unknowingly contribute to a child's anger with unhelpful responses. A common example of this would be when parents give double messages to their children. A parent might say: "I'm so happy that you came to supper on time. Once in a year isn't bad." There are parents who find it quite difficult to give a straight compliment to their child, and find that such painful comments are easier to verbalize. When looking at his angry child, the parent needs to introspect and consider the possible part that he himself may be playing, as well.

Once an adult verbally shifts the cause of a child's pain to an external or accidental cause, anger and aggression may also be reduced in a child. A parent needs to listen to his child speak, with an open mind, and attack the problem, not the person, as it has been stated previously. A parent can ask: "What's another way that I can handle this?" or "This has helped me in the past. I hope that it can help you."

In reality, constructive parenting techniques are sometimes created due to the challenges of angry children. One needs to judge each circumstance, depending on the specific needs of the child, in the particular stage of his development. Again, teaching appropriate coping mechanisms is perhaps the greatest gift that we can give our children.

The mistrustful child — constantly needing reassurance from others, and self-reassurance

22

OFTENTIMES, PARENTS FIND it puzzling to have a child who seems to be mistrustful by nature. Sometimes a parent will uncomfortably admit that he too is mistrustful and that the child absorbed this maladaptive coping mechanism. Others find that their child is generally more mistrustful and cynical, and it affects his openness to new ideas and new people. A parent may easily be frustrated when such a child is continually closed towards others and suspects peoples' motives continually.

When we learn the *halachos* of *shemiras halashon*, we see the concept of "*kabdeihu v'chashdeihu*." This is the idea that if a person has reason to doubt another person's integrity, he should still give the person proper respect, but yet be on guard with the person. Thus, some cynicism is warranted in certain occasions, and should be applied for our self-preservation. Throughout our lives, much of our actions are clearly "calculated risks," as we weigh and measure our actions according to the information we have at our disposal at the time. However, very few great achievements in our world would have occurred if it were not for the fact that some risk factor was involved, and the person chose to take that risk. This concept needs to be stressed with a mistrustful child. If a person does not take a "calculated risk," certain opportunities in life will not reoccur, and the person may not have the chance to use the same potential and possibly rise to the occasion.

This idea is seen in *Megillas Esther*, when Mordechai asks Esther to plead for the Jews, and this calculated risk saved all of us. Hashem rules the world and only He can know how events will turn out in any given situation. An appropriate amount of trust towards other people needs to be seen through the role-modeling of one's parents. A child also needs to see that no person has the ultimate ability to hurt another, if Hashem does not desire that this occur. In this way, the issue of mistrust will be decreased, and the child's potential as a human being will not to be stifled due to continual fear of others.

Working with my perfectionist child — making mistakes 23

SOME CHILDREN HAVE great difficulty in dealing with the reality of human imperfection — and with their own imperfection, in particular. Such children may erase part of their drawing numerous times and feel quite frustrated, not feeling comfortable with the picture's final outcome. Not achieving the desired masterpiece can be very disappointing for such a child.

Another child might be fearful of not knowing the correct answer in class, and would rather not answer (or daydream), rather than be embarrassed by answering his teacher incorrectly. This child may not appear to be a perfectionist, and may not be so exacting in many areas of his life, but in the areas where this child does have these feelings, his frustration tolerance is very limited.

It is written that: "*Ein tzaddik ba'aretz asher ya'aseh tov v'lo yecheta*" (there is no *tzaddik* that has lived without committing a transgression). A person can still be consumed by destructive guilt due to his various human foibles. If a child seems to suffer from such sentiments, a parent needs to remind the child that: "Even Moshe Rabbeinu made a mistake. Do you think that you're greater than Moshe?"

A parent might need to verbalize how he himself may have made a mistake that day and how reparations were made. (Clearly, in order to maintain respect for one's parent, the mistake verbalized should be a minor one, and not be said in a manner of confession to one's child.) However, the idea of rectifying one's mistakes is an integral concept in a person's life, and one that can be introduced in the life of a child at quite a young age.

A parent can color with a child in a coloring book, and intentionally color the people's faces green or purple, and laugh at how people can also have make-believe face color. A parent can also color out of the line slightly, to get the point across to such a child that every page in the book doesn't have to be perfect.

A parent can also have a discussion with his child about how this perfectionist attitude seems to be making him quite sad. A parent and child need to problem-solve ways to deal with such thoughts as: "I'm supposed to get everything right. What's going on here?" A parent may ask his child: "Are such thoughts helping you to try harder, or just to feel sad?" "What other thoughts can you think about that can really help you?" is another possible question that can be asked.

Most importantly, a parent has to scrutinize his own behavior, and be sure that he himself is not being a role model for perfectionism. A child learns coping mechanisms best (both healthy and faulty) from those people closest to them. Modeling our own helpful ways of coping is an invaluable tool for our children.

24 *The stubborn child*

IT IS OFTEN said that being strong-willed can be an asset in one's life. Great people are driven to lofty ideals and high aspirations through their determination. However, strong-willed people also need to learn to be flexible. And as a parent, this is a skill that one can teach one's child.

In reality, being one out of many siblings is an asset for a stubborn child. If such a child was an only child, it would only be more difficult for him to acclimate to society-at-large. He would constantly wonder why things didn't go his way and would be angry at the prospect of change, or things constantly being out of his control. Learning to share is an important developmental task for all children, especially stubborn ones.

A parent needs to always attempt to be consistent with children, but even more so with a stubborn child. A stubborn child will corner you with your inconsistencies, and find that opening in order to crawl in and get his way! And if a person does weaken to the demands of a stubborn child due to incessant whining and crying, this will only broaden the child's future pathways to more whining and crying (if he succeeded once, why not attempt it again?).

Though a parent should not easily capitulate to the demands of a child, one should not be excessively demanding either, as a means to put a child in his place. In this way, one would be exemplifying a role model of a stubborn demanding parent (which is the least desirable role model one wants to reflect to such a child). One should rather make a statement in a more controlled manner (closer to a neutral stance, rather than showing much emotion). For in this way, a parent clarifies who the authority is, and whose opinion will be final, without creating an emotion-filled confrontation.

Avoiding confrontation with an overly responsive child is an important constructive preventative measure. This doesn't mean that a parent hides toys or candy as a way of preventing a child from demanding them. A child need not be protected from hearing: "Everything I want, I cannot receive." This is crucial for a child to learn.

Avoiding confrontation is accomplished by parents who watch how they speak. Some parents know how easily they can put someone "against the wall," as it is colloquially expressed. Stubborn children are challenged by statements expressing ultimatums and severe threats, and feel that a parent almost enters into a power struggle with them, when spoken to in such a manner. A person needs to give children limitations and guidelines, but one's tone of voice can reflect the differences between limitations and ultimatums.

Adolescents by nature are often very stubborn, as a means of asserting their independence. The skill of negotiation and problem-solving is a technique most successfully applied with strong-willed individuals, and often a daily necessity applied for teenagers. Even if your child is still young, there are times when problem-solving techniques are very helpful and are definitely not in the category of spoiling a child. A child learns that he can redirect his desires and someone else's desires, and someone else's desires can be responded to, as well. Both parent and child jointly discuss what they desire and attempt to brainstorm ideas that could possibly lead to more of a compromise. (Problem-solving, however, should be used for major issues that do not seem to be resolving themselves. It is not to be used on a continual basis for a child's every request.)

As in all situations with children, the ability to give praise cannot be underestimated. A stubborn child whose self-esteem is worked with will be able to be flexible more easily. If one is more inwardly secure, one will be more able to listen to the other, as the changing world around him will be less of a threat. Thus, he will be less stubborn in his responses and reactions to other individuals. Inner security is created when one's self-esteem is strengthened. In general, there is no more important endeavor of a parent than attempting to build a child's self-esteem.

The fearful child 25

THE WAY OF response to a fearful child differs, depending on the many variables involved in his given situation. Initially, a parent needs to analyze the possible cause of the existing fear, and ask open-ended questions to his child, to better explore the nature of the problem. An open-ended question is one where the respondent is unable to answer "yes" or "no," and needs to be more verbally descriptive in his response. An example of this might be: "What kind of things are on your mind when you can't fall asleep at night?" A child can shrug his shoulders, but a parent can use his mutual-storytelling abilities to try and elicit information from the child.

This type of questioning can stimulate some introspection on the child's part, and instill a belief that the problem/ fear can be resolved. When a parent shares an experience from his own childhood with his child (which may strike a chord in the heart of the child), he can then describe appropriate coping mechanisms related to the experience. This reassures a fearful child that his fears and anxieties can be resolved and overcome. By attempting to understand a child's fears, one can help to "detoxify" the negative experience by dissecting the actual fear when speaking together with the child. One can show that its actual power and hold is imaginary, externalizing its effect upon the child. For example, a parent can look for the feared imaginary monkeys in the backyard with a flashlight together with his child. Instead of the fear existing in the heart of the child, the monkeys are confronted in the backyard (and then, never to be found).

One can either problem-solve or confront the issue of fear, depending on its severity. Confrontation in relation to the child's anxiety can be gradual, or more direct, depending on the child's personality and the factors involved. Clearly, in this area and all areas of parenting, professional help needs to be sought when a parent is unable to go at certain tasks alone. In general, once a fear is outside of yourself, it is something that you feel can be conquered, and has much less weight upon the soul.

According to Harav Eliyahu Dessler *zt"l*, in *Michtav MeEliyahu*, this is seen with Adam Harishon with the *Etz Hadaas*. He initially envisioned the *yetzer hara* as something outside of himself. It had no bearing on his idyllic life. Once he ate from the tree, he internalized the concept of evil that was previously outside of him — this undesirable existence was something that he (and all people) now needed to battle with on a daily basis.

In a similar vein, if we can externalize what is bothering our child, its power will not have such a strong impact upon our child. Being able to dissect a fear over and over with a child can take away issues of anxiety. Once a person has externalized its power — something outside of him can be examined and worked with more easily — the problem then becomes re-workable. A child needs to identify his existence with a sense of competency and control, as guided by his parents' continual belief in him.

The oppositional child 26

MUCH HAS BEEN written on the topic of the opposi-tional child, but techniques often deal with working with the child's given limitations, rather than focusing on her future potential. A counselor might advise a child to deal with a teacher's personality by trying not to get him-self "caught," rather than seeing the child's future potential working together with a teacher and classmates. This initial approach is quite understandable, as an oppositional child is often quite guarded, and is used to being offensive in response to authority. However, one needs to follow the approach of Chassidic philosophy, stressing the *neshamah's* endless potential and how our positive thoughts can some-times aid this process. A parent needs to possess a belief in the child's eventual ability to acclimate appropriately to the world around him.

Since an oppositional child doesn't often receive a straight message comfortably — be it a compliment or a direct request — a parent needs to speak in a more para-doxical round-about manner to achieve desirable results. A parent can use humor in getting a point across, saying: "I think that Sara is hiding — the Sara I know wouldn't say such a thing to her brother," and then proceed to search for her daughter in the living room. In a similar vein, a parent can say: "Do you think that I am so silly to think that you're not a good girl? I know better than that!" or "Do you think that you can fool me into thinking that you're not a good girl? I know that you did x and y this morning!" Since these are not direct statements, they can be received much easier by oppositional children.

One can sometimes problem-solve quite successfully with such children, if the parameters of solutions and suggestions involved are extremely clear, and these ideas allow for optional alternative plans (if the initial endeavors fail). Optional plans allow for the unexpected, and adults' limitations, so that the oppositional child will have less reason to be angered, as her expectations will be more realistic. Some children's responses are more tempered, and they are more responsive to adults when certain difficult issues are explained to them, as well. Some oppositional behavior is due to lack of understanding, when certain children are expected to obey, without sufficient understanding of a difficult circumstance that confronts them.

A parent needs to expend a great amount of energy in an effort to avoid responding in a defensive manner to an oppositional child (though this is a natural initial response). Once a power struggle begins, there are no victors in this battle. As such a child's behavior is stemming from a variety of factors, a parent's response needs to be varied, as well. One response might be due to a child's low frustration tolerance, and another might be due to a child's intense issue of sibling rivalry. A parent needs to attempt to vary his responses, depending on the given situation.

A parent also needs to try preventive measures to avoid power struggles. If a parent is aware of possible issues that might emerge in a given situation, it needs to be spoken about, to avoid unnecessary stress with the oppositional child. The stance that a parent needs to project is that of compassion and sensitivity towards his child, and not a fear of the child's possible volatile response. A parent can sense if his child's behavior has become a manipulative tactic, or is a cry to be understood. To prevent this pattern from becoming a negative one, a parent needs to be patient and compassionate, and not fearful and defensive. Avoiding power struggles is clearly a continual challenge when working with such children.

Dealing with the ADHD child — positive reinforcement and structure 27

IMPULSIVE BEHAVIOR (AS discussed above) is only a partial description of an ADHD child. There are other bio-chemical factors that play a part in this diagnosis, and which need to be understood, in order to work better with such a child. The two most important factors in helping an ADHD child behaviorally is that of creating structure in the child's schedule, and giving positive reinforcement for his various commendable achievements.

As discussed previously, natural consequences of negative actions are not perceived easily by certain children. Thus, again we see that an ADHD child must see and understand the consequences of his actions, but he will not necessarily learn from negative behavioral consequences. Positive reinforcement has proven to be the most effective form of behavior modification for ADHD children.

Giving structure to a child that doesn't create his own natural structure is similar to giving a navigation system to a sailor with a directional disability.

The origin of ADHD (Attention Deficit and Hyper-activity Disorder) is not yet clear, but it is a problem that can definitely be helped by modifying certain behavioral conditions in a child's environment. Some parents find that decreasing a child's intake of sugar is helpful, but this has not always been proven statistically. Testing helps to clarify if a child does have this condition, or any other possible learning disability that may be an impediment to a child's learning. By testing and determining the severity of the disorder, a parent can help judge what seems best for his child. If a child's behavior is severely disrupting his classmates' learning, or severely disrupting his own learning, the possibility of using medication to help the child's condition may need to be explored.

However, in general, a parent needs to initially work with a child's environment in order to work with the child's natural inclination to be distracted. Children such as these need much positive reinforcement and structure. As they become so easily distracted and find it difficult to be "down to earth," the definite beginnings and ends of activities add a sense of security to the world around them. Emphasizing time limits and using timers are other examples of giving structure to children.

Immediate rewards for positive actions are what are needed in relation to positive reinforcement. The goals for such children should be small goals, as large goals may seem insurmountable for children who seem to view life as quick fleeting moments on a screen. These children (like all children) need consequences for their negative behavior. Yet these children generally respond less to punishment than to reward. These children often see punishment as a criticism of their very personality make-up — especially if their punishments are inconsistent and unstructured.

If a parent or teacher only punishes a child for disruptive behavior, this punishment is unlikely to have a long-lasting effect on the child. They would accomplish more by complimenting the child's understanding of the *parashah* in front of family members, and changing the child's view of himself as always being "the problem." This is perhaps the greatest challenge in dealing with such children: the ability of a parent to have patience after seeing continual disruptive behavior, and constantly redirecting the child to short-term goals with rewards.

ADHD children are often not attuned to social cues, which is obviously no fault of their own. Being easily distracted makes it difficult to know which human interactions are most important to respond to. Thus, teachers do not necessarily find a great emotional connection with these children, as they may feel slighted that the "child never listens to me."

Another helpful idea for teachers is the often-used placing the child in front of the teacher — allowing for less distraction on the part of the child. Other often helpful ideas are that of giving ADHD children more active jobs in the classroom, such as being board monitor or going to the school office on errands. In general, the reward system that one uses at home can be similarly implemented at school. A child can be rewarded for properly being part of a class, and then use segments of times in school (as in a chart created for a one-hour task performance) to work on a more-individual level.

If, however, a child misbehaves, a teacher doesn't need to remark or write a zero on a star-chart, or write a berating report about the child's lack of attention. A child needs to receive a consequence for his action, but what he achieved until now still belongs to him. (This concept is explained at more length in Pathways #31.) Counseling can be very beneficial for helping the child to acclimate to his world, aside from the family's need for him to function better within the family unit.

In relation to a child's ability to concentrate on electronic games for long periods of time — this is not necessarily a sign that a child does not have ADHD. An intensive relaxing activity can be a great release for a sidetracked child — almost a restful island in a fast-moving world.

If one were to examine the childhood history of many great doers in our world, a sizable portion of this group might easily have been diagnosed as having Attention Deficit Disorder. What caused them to be successful in their endeavors was a rechanneling of their great energies into admirable pursuits and actions. May this be the direction that your child follows and all those whose potentials need to be developed, each in their own unique way.

28 A parent's response to selective mutism in her child

THE MOST COMMON form of anxiety in a preschool child is that of selective mutism. The degree of selective mutism may vary in each given circumstance — some children will only speak to their teacher in school, some only to their peers, some will sing but not speak, etc.

It is quite difficult for a parent not to show her discomfort with this behavior, but it is of paramount importance for a parent not to exhibit disappointment and anxiety about this issue. As always, anxiety breeds anxiety, and a parent needs to internalize the realistic belief that the child will eventually speak more openly in class. A parent needs to refrain from bringing up the topic to her child's teacher when she picks up her preschooler each day.

What a parent can attempt to do is to work around the problem, rather than continually speaking about it openly. A child can be rewarded for *davening* in school, stressing how it makes Hashem so happy, or "you sound just like your Totty" (not focusing on the issue of not hearing his voice). A child can *daven* at home and be taped and bring it to school, if the child is self-conscious about *davening* in school. A parent first needs to ask permission to have the child's voice taped, perhaps asking later if it's okay to bring the tape to school.

A child can have a classmate come to her home after school to play. This sometimes opens a conversation which can continue the next day in school. A child can come to her teacher's house on Shabbos with her siblings (whom she may possibly speak to), to help open that possibility of communication. A child can have her class birthday party at home (with her permission, of course), if that can assist the process of decreasing her anxiety towards classmates.

Sometimes a teacher can use a microphone, and go around the room giving the children who want to, an opportunity to speak into the microphone. Sometimes a borderline selective mute might be caught off guard, and hear his voice in the microphone. When a child does speak, a fuss should not be made. A child does not want to be the center of attention. (Incidentally, his classmates will do the job for you! They will be quite enthusiastic to hear his voice, and excitedly tell the teacher.)

As selective mutism is connected to feelings of anxiety and feeling uncertain, a parent needs to work on this child's feelings of competency and self-esteem, to help him feel secure about the world around him. Some selectively mute children are perfectionists, and would rather not speak than say something silly or incorrect. In such a circumstance, one needs to work on the child's issues of never being able to make a mistake, in order to give him the confidence to make a mistake one day in his classroom.

Other children might fear their bellowing *rebbi's* voice, or internalize problematic issues that are occurring at home, and feel more frightened in class. A parent needs to spend moments of "being silly" together with his child, to allow the child to see that even adults can take life lightly, at times. The acceptance of the child during this temporary stage in his life, and not broadcasting his selective mutism as a public announcement to others, is also of great importance in working with this issue. If asked, a parent needs to say: "She'll speak when she's ready. Thanks."

29 Parents' involvement with a child "on the spectrum" of PDD

CHILDREN WITH ISSUES of Pervasive Developmental Disorder (PDD) vary in the degree of their intensity and limitations. Clearly, children with autism are at one extreme of the spectrum, and their treatment is very specific, depending on the theoretic framework that is applied in each given case. That issue is not being discussed at this point. These ideas are more focused towards young children who exhibit milder degrees of PDD. These children may be helped by a parent's involvement and assistance from various therapists during the initial years of their life.

Children who seem to be too self-absorbed and have limited social skills can be worked with through continual engagement in conversations, requesting eye contact with their parent. A parent can stress how they love to see the child's beautiful brown eyes — but where are they? One can ask an opinion of a four- or five-year-old, and expect appropriate affect, and not accept a monotone voice when given a response. A parent can say: "I don't hear the *lebedig* Miriam that I know and love!"

A parent needs to have a dialogue with such a child (even when the verbal response is limited) to show that ideas are discussed and thought about with others. Parents need to discuss fears — a major component of children with PDD — in order to allow the children's involvement in everyday life to be more comfortable and less frightening. A parent needs to offer solutions to fearful situations that she has found herself in, to help reassure her child that she, too, can overcome her fears.

A parent can use positive-reinforcement charts to help motivate such a child to attempt new tasks or initiate conversation with classmates. Extra points are received for maintaining eye contact, or not repeating certain statements continually (which is a hallmark sign of a PDD child).

Although the techniques mentioned here are often used with therapists at school, a wise parent can implement similar initiatives at home, to help reinforce changes that her child needs to make in order to integrate more successfully into mainstream social situations.

PARENTS' EMOTIONAL RESPONSES TO THEIR CHILDREN

Being consistent when you can't be — the "saving face clause" 30

ONE CANNOT UNDERESTIMATE the importance of attempting to create a sense of consistency for a child — especially for a very young child. Such a child needs to feel a sense of security in an ever-changing world. If children generally know what to expect in a given situation at home, their view of life and the world-at-large is more solidified, even at an early age. Many parents complain that they can't be consistent, as they are forgetful due to their ever-changing schedule ("I forgot the punishment/reward that I promised), and give up on even attempting to be consistent.

A parent needs to attempt to be consistent, and then maintain a sense of dignity and be flexible to change, responding differently to one's child when the situation warrants change. This is similar to the Asian concept of "saving face," when the situation changes beyond one's control.

An example of this would be putting off the consequence of "time-out" to a more workable time (i.e. due to an unexpected guest, or an impending appointment). Though a parent may complain that they will forget to dispense the consequence at another time, a child has to see some attempt at a parent being consistent. It is preferable to write a note on a refrigerator to remind a parent (even if it falls off). If appropriate, a parent may verbalize the need to be flexible (clarifying that this is not inconsistency). One can say: "I'm not going to lose out on time today because you have to go in time-out. Then that becomes a punishment for the entire family. Yet when we go out today, you'll get an orange instead of ice cream." Though certain parents get distracted more easily and don't always follow through on punishments and rewards, children of such parents need to see such attempts (such as putting yellow sticky papers on the wall), to see that it is everyone's job to work on their character flaws — their parent's job, as well as theirs.

One way of "saving face" is that of having a list available of possible negative consequences for actions (either in one's mind, or written on paper), to use with your children when your desirable "consequence of action" is unworkable. A creative example of this is utilizing "cleaning lady time." A child can owe his parent "cleaning lady time," to do extra household chores, as a consequence of his negative behavior. A parent can calculate the amount of time spent as a result of the child's aggravating behavior, and charge cleaning time by the hour. "You caused me not to be able to complete things in the house. The cleaning lady now has to do it. That's nine dollars an hour that you owe me, for an hour and a half of non-completed work." In this way, a child sees a "rhyme and reason" to change, through a parent's response to him.

31 Appreciating the child who is hard to appreciate

CERTAIN CHILDREN SEEM to be more difficult for particular parents to work with. These children's personalities seem to rub parents the wrong way. A parent feels frustrated and guilty at the same time. Since a parent puts so much effort into child-rearing, when a child's behavioral outcomes are problematic, a parent feels a great sense of disappointment and guilt. One may ask the dramatic question: "Where did I go wrong?" Besides frustration and anger in relation to the child with the problematic outcome, one can experience a great sense of failure in one's role as a parent.

If a parent can go beyond his initial anger and disappointment with the problematic outcome of a specific child, he is able to facilitate emotional and psychological growth. In order to do this, a parent needs to be honest and ask, "What is the message being sent to this child?" Is it the message: "You rub me the wrong way? You're obnoxious, bossy, and you don't even do much in yeshivah..."? Such a parent almost seems to have lost hope in the possibility of any change in his son's behavior while he is living at home. A child must sense this. A parent needs to ask himself: "Am I able to find any redeeming quality in my child?" If you can barely find any (or you have, and you barely verbalize it to him), it would be very difficult for him to see redeeming qualities within himself.

One first needs to think of the Divine Providence in this unique challenge of being *mechanech* this particular child. And if within every child there is the opportunity for growth, how can a parent grow and improve his *middos* under such circumstances?

It is interesting to note how Rivka Imeinu dealt with the "worst child" that one can possibly imagine. After Yitzchak gave the blessings to Yaakov and Esav, we find an interesting commentary on the words: "Rivka the mother of Yaakov and Esav." Why is this phrase mentioned at a time when Yitzchak is sending Yaakov to find a wife? We are already aware of this information. One commentary suggests that although Rivka saw the evil within Esav and helped Yaakov win the blessings, telling him to go far away from Esav to save his life (and find a wife), Esav was still her son. Her identity was the mother of both children.

Sometimes a parent needs to be very strict when it comes to discipline. Unconditional tolerance of any negative behavior that a child exhibits is not a constructive approach. This can be seen in relation to Avshalom and Esav. Both their parents (Dovid Hamelech and Yitzchak respectively) tolerated their negative behavior, feeling that if they were too strict, these two sons would surely rebel. Some commentators feel that the fathers' lack of strong discipline helped create the children's downfall. In this case, severity from one's parents may have been helpful. One also sees how Yishmael had to be driven out of Avraham's house in order not to have a bad influence on Yitzchak. Though severity is sometimes necessary, one should consult with a competent Torah authority to determine when such behavior is appropriate.

Generally speaking, however, as mentioned in the *Gemara*, it has been many generations since people could actually give or receive rebuke effectively, and today, the more "positive view" towards a child has been most successful in creating positive character traits. At first glance, you may respond: "How can I react positively to *middos* that I find reprehensible?"

According to the Baal Shem Tov, if you are particularly bothered by another person's negative character trait, it is a very strong possibility that you possess that same trait. We identify with such a trait because we know it only too well. This is especially true between parents and children. Hashem gives children character traits that are similar to the parents', so that a parent can feel a natural affinity to his children. As a person gains the capability of working with his *middos*, he can pass this knowledge to his children who have similar tendencies (both positive and negative). However, a parent can sometimes over-identify with his child's negative traits, actually becoming angry when he observes these undesirable traits, both with himself and his child. Thus, a parent needs to be honest with himself so that he can understand who he is truly disappointed in. According to Reb Nachman of Breslov, this problem can be viewed in another way. He looked at the words from *Tehillim* and he looked carefully at the evil person, and he no longer existed (*Tehillim* 37, 10). Reb Nachman understood this as a way to elevate other human beings spiritually. A person must meditate upon this "evil" person, and if he truly meditates on any of this person's positive traits, he will no longer be a *rasha* (an evil person). If a person looks for one good point and another good point (through great thought and giving the benefit of the doubt to the child involved), his feelings will change, causing the child's vision of himself to improve. If a parent verbalizes the details of a child's good points, how much more meaningful will this be to a child's sense of self. Thus, a parent needs to mold a child's self-esteem, which will give an unruly child the potential to change and improve his behavior.

One way of molding a child's self-esteem is by establishing a time that one or both parents spend alone with him. However often these meetings may be, a child will begin to feel that his company is very desirable and he is enjoyable to be with. A child will generally not have the need to seek attention through negative means if a parent helps emphasize a child's personal talent in which he excels. This talent can be in any area, or it can be created as in excellence in certain areas of *chessed*. Through this vehicle, a child's self-esteem and satisfaction within himself can be fulfilled.

32 Which children benefit (and do not benefit) from "natural consequences"

VERY OFTEN CERTAIN teachers feel that students only learn from their mistakes, and stress this form of student "self-education." An example of this might be allowing a child to see what results from coming late. A ride might leave without him, or he might lose the trust and relationship of a friend. Though many people understand definite rewards and punishments — are they irritating enough to this particular child to motivate him to change? The natural consequences of their limitations often don't seem to faze certain types of children. What type of child are we referring to?

There are three types of children who seem to disregard "natural consequences." The child who is non-conventional and often marches to his own drum is one such child. He will find an alternative plan to achieve his desired ends, and not get too ruffled by his need to acclimate to his existing environment. The second type of child is the child with low self-esteem. This child has limited expectations, and is not surprised that he has no snack again, and doesn't expect things to change or to improve greatly. He is not disregarding his teacher or parent when making the same mistakes, but his mind is preoccupied with his self-image and how he fits (or doesn't fit) into the world around him. The third child is the child that may be too imaginative and day-dreamy, and doesn't focus so easily. An ADD child might fit into this category.

Such children avoid feelings of being severely embarrassed by not following rules, because "they didn't hear you anyway."

Instead of being continually disappointed in the above-mentioned children, one needs to realize that this method is not effective for all types of children. These children are more readily motivated by positive reinforcement, as this can improve their self-esteem. Such children (and adults) would choose a desirable reward and even leave their pleasant daydreams for a possible desired outcome, gained through a positive-reinforcement system. These children, however, still need to be shown the consequences of their actions in order to understand how our world operates. These consequences may not necessarily change their behavior (as we see on a daily basis with the child who continually gets negative consequences for his behavior). What is more effective instead is using motivational techniques to work on each one of these particular children's behavioral challenges.

Dealing with guilt — the "never-good-enough mom/dad" 33

IN OUR GENERATION, the ability to make an accurate "self-accounting" of ourselves is a very challenging proposition. People are apt to fall into depression when focusing on their shortcomings, and tend to overlook their many worthwhile capabilities. "Beating yourself up" is a common expression that we hear which describes how people are often very hard on themselves. People generally do not appreciate the good that they possess, either due to false humility or an over-scrupulous self-analysis. They can easily recount the mistakes that they amassed on a given day, but cannot recall their small contributions that they gave to the world around them on that day.

The Baal Shem Tov speaks of a person's need to possess two pockets — one with the idea that "*bishvili nivra haolam*" (the world was created for me). In the other pocket we possess the idea that "*anochi afar va'eifer*" (I am but dust and ashes). One needs to envision the power of any given moment — the world was created for the individual alone — and yet see that we are still as a speck in the ocean in relation to this world and lifetimes that have passed. If I have truly thought about my parenting abilities and ways to improve them, and worked on my *middos*, and *davened* for *siyatta diShmaya* for the job to be one of excellence, there is no need for self-flagellation. If these feelings do occur, it is most likely the work of the ever-ready evil inclination, who finds great gratification when humans fall into depression. People are generally not motivated to improve, due to depression and feeling sorry for themselves. If anything, *timtum halev* (literally "a stuffing up of the heart") is often caused by such self-destructive thought, as discussed by Rav Dessler and many other *ba'alei machshavah*.

Parents often look back at previous parenting mistakes with guilt and discomfort, and can feel quite discouraged. However, human beings only make decisions with the limited information that is momentarily placed before them, and are judged according to these factors. "If we only knew..." are words that may resonate unceasingly in our minds. However, if Hashem wanted us to know certain information, this information would have been revealed to us.

One can see a clear example of this in the *Gemara* (a tractate customarily read on Tishah B'Av): Rabbi Zecharia ben Avkulis objected to accepting a sacrifice that had been offered by the Caesar which had an invalidating blemish. He thus inadvertently set into motion a chain of events that resulted in the destruction of the Second Beis Hamikdash. Yet he is not called a murderer or destroyer, as his motivation was to preserve with clarity the criteria for determining which animals were suitable to be offered as sacrifices in the Temple (see *Gittin* 56a). He had no premonition that his action would have such devastating ramifications.

We too are judged by our actions, not by all the unanticipated ripple effects that may result from them. When one is motivated *l'shem Shamayim* (involving *da'as Torah* when necessary) and makes use of the information that is accessible, one does not carry culpability, even if the outcome proves to be negative.

Thus, the never-being- "good-enough" parent only gives up on his task more easily when challenged, as he feels: "Anyway, it will never really be good enough..." A parent's true humility reflects the realization that we always have more to give, and we are not yet fully utilizing our potential. It is this idea that can inspire us to do more, as we realize that we indeed possess the potential to meet this and all challenges. If Hashem gives us challenges "*lifi kocho*" — each challenge is given to each one who can manage it — then this too is within our reach.

Avoiding putting children into roles — self-fulfilling prophecy   34

A N UNFORTUNATE TRUISM that we often encounter is that of people fulfilling negative "prophecies" delivered by their parents throughout their childhood. "If you act like this, no one normal will marry you" is such a statement that one may hear. If such a statement is heard continually, one may unconsciously have self-doubts about her ability to marry someone of worth. On a date one may even see a possible future spouse's severe character flaw (such as anger), but then make little of it, as she envisions herself as being quite flawed, as well.

This is also true in terms of parents who create positive roles for their children. By putting a child into a specific role (even though this role may seem to be a positive one — as the "smart one"), one is somewhat boxed into a role that one cannot always achieve. One cannot always get marks in the 90's, and one is not always in the mood to be almost perfect either. A parent can give specific compliments about a child's achievements (as this is most helpful in building self-esteem), but be flexible and easygoing enough in tone, to not make this description a never-ending expectation on the part of a parent. She would rather be seen as a complete human being, with strengths and weaknesses, and loved unconditionally by her parents.

35 *Corporeal punishment — spare the rod?*

ALL TOO OFTEN, parents think that they are responding consistently, by threatening to give a "*potch*" whenever disobedience is sensed. We live in a world where corporeal punishment is shunned; a child views hitting differently in this generation than he would in previous generations. Most often, a child sees a parent as losing control, rather than understanding that he is being punished, when he gets hit. One may attempt to shun the permissive society around us, and feel that this treatment was "good enough for us. Why should it not be good enough for our children?" After all, many people of the previous generation lived with such an upbringing, and seem to be basically well-adjusted.

This point can be argued. However, more practically speaking, enough children see their peers being appropriately disciplined without hitting, so that their own hitting parents seem quite intense and lacking self-control, in contrast to the calmer parents. How many parents actually feign anger to get across a point to their children (as the Rambam requires in relation to *chinuch*) rather than being in an actual state of anger? How many parents actually hit their child, but don't feel anger within them? When being hit, a child clearly experiences a parent's rage, losing respect for the parent, as a child rarely focuses on the reason that he is being hit. When adults, too, feel that we are unjustly blamed (or attacked verbally), we generally focus on the attacker, and not the actual fault that they find with us.

Children will focus on the aggressive and sometimes violent behavior, and often equate religion with their parents (or their *rebbeim* in yeshivah), rejecting the entire package. We live in a world where we are a button away from a hedonistic and "everything is okay" society. When the pressure becomes too intense, who needs to stay around for more?

If a parent truly wants ways to decrease negative behaviors, there are various methods available, besides various methods to encourage positive behavior. Intense rage gives certain parents a sense of an adrenaline rush, and they feel invigorated in a destructive fashion. Thus, such a parent may continue to respond to his child in rage, though he knows that its effects can truly be disastrous.

In general, violence breeds violence, and when a person with power (in this case, a parent) uses physical expression to reflect this power (to his child), a child will exhibit similar behavior towards peers and siblings.

One needs to truly be honest in one's method of discipline, and speak to Rabbanim to ascertain whether one's method of discipline is appropriate. Rav Wolbe *shlita* writes in *Alei Shor* that the often spoken of "rod" mentioned in the Torah was a thin strap, one that barely caused pain. When we speak of not sparing the rod, the rod was not a belt or a slipper, or whatever an out-of-control parent might find in a room.

If a parent desires to make a point about safety to a small child — for example, after a child runs across the street and doesn't watch for cars, or after a child plays with matches — hitting a child one time on his hand can make a strong impression on a child. In such a circumstance, since such a parent never hits his child, the lesson about safety will not be forgotten by the child. Such an action is clearly not an act of rage, but an expression of warning and concern from a devoted parent.

The *Gemara* states that in the generation before Moshiach, *chutzpah* will be rampant. This challenge is one that all parents in our generation deal with on a daily basis. What is considered by some as honest communication between parent and child is considered by others as *chutzpah*. A parent needs to improve communication with his children to avoid unnecessary confrontations which only separate parent and child.

Another cause for parental guilt — Did I give enough? Was I too withholding? 36

DEPENDING ON ONE'S culture, each parent has a view of what it means to be giving to a child. Whether it is giving of one's time, of one's patience, or of one's monetary abilities, each parent has a general idea of what he needs to give to his children. In some families, parents feel guilty when closing children out of their bedroom and others feel guilty when they cannot give an allowance to their children. Some parents are very apologetic if they cannot spend much time talking to their children, due to scheduling difficulties. On the other hand, some parents feel guilty about hardly anything that they do, and should perhaps be more honest in evaluating what their parenting responsibilities are!

In reality, our society tends to be overindulgent when it comes to giving to children. One's child desires an Ipod — "Why not? It will help him relax," a parent might say. Another child might desire additional expensive items that a particular family might find very difficult to afford. One child may want to talk to her mother for a half an hour every night, and this may be close to impossible in relation to her mother's schedule. The guilt that many parents experience in such circumstances needs to be scrutinized.

If a child receives all that she presently desires in her life from her parents, this can surely be a set-up for disaster. She will be continually disappointed throughout her life if she feels that unconditional love is equivalent to getting all her desires fulfilled.

No human being can ever actually fulfill all our desires, and it is only Hashem who is capable of such complete giving. In fact, this capacity for Ultimate *chessed* is not yet to be revealed in our finite world, as we experience it (as explained in *Chovos Halevavos*).

In truth, many people are depressed in their adult life, because no one is giving to them as their parents did. The boss at work has definite expectations, and a worker receives consequences for not living up to these expectations. A spouse similarly has certain expectations and is disappointed when one's behavior is not as desired. Thus, the child-like desire of always "getting what you want" can really never be satiated (even as a child).

This is especially true when one enters adult life. Although many parents might say: "I want my children to get everything now. The world is so cruel," this thinking is faulty. A child needs to acclimate to this world by seeing the limitations of every human being now, so he won't be continually disappointed by others in years to come. If parents do experience guilt, perhaps it should be from the fact that they didn't teach their children appropriate coping mechanisms, rather than because they did not give their children everything that they desired.

37 *Creative ways for families to work with the child that "doesn't fit in"*

OFTENTIMES, FAMILIES CAN find themselves with a child who doesn't fit the mold of the family. The child can be non-conventional in a conventional family, or the opposite situation can exist. A child can be more materialistically-inclined than most family members, and feel misunderstood and judged. A wise parent needs to balance the needs of the individual with the needs of the family unit.

Sometimes such a child feels more comfortable with one parent, and can confide in that parent more. This parent needs to stress the family's acceptance of differences, and how this parent feels that this individuality is special. "As there are many flowers in a garden, are there various types of family members living in this house." Such a child can get easily frustrated with family members, and even wish to be in another family. Parents need to stress that it is with *Hashgachah Pratis* that each person is part of a particular family. Each member has something to share and give, in order that each can learn from each other's talents and good *middos*.

Both parents need to verbally stress the good points of this "out-of-sync" sibling to family members, in order that this child's self-esteem won't be severely affected. A parent needs to remind siblings that what they might look at as weird or fanatic in their sibling's personality actually can be very helpful in certain circumstances. A parent needs to give specific examples, in order that siblings learn to be less judgmental by seeing the "*nekudos tovos*" (good points) of their unique sibling. A parent needs to also stress similarities on a continual basis, pointing out what cements family members together. Warm family memories and shared family philosophies often bring diverse family members together.

Suggesting that this child is similar to one's parents or in-laws is also a way of cementing similarities, and allows the child to feel less "out of things." Besides the need for food, water and air, the need to belong to something is of utmost importance to human beings. Feeling that they are an important part of a family is an integral need for most human beings. Creating family jokes and pleasant ways of relating to each other also accentuates similarities, and creates more of an environment of acceptance. As one's home is a microcosm of the world, one needs to use all of its resources in order to serve Hashem, incorporating all of its aspects, no matter how diversified and complex it may seem.

SPIRITUAL
CONCERNS

Helping to instill spirituality in your children 38

WHEN THE KOTZKER Rebbe first went to the Maggid of Mezritch and became a chassid, his parents were very dismayed. They asked him what he learned from the chassidim that he didn't learn from his previous yeshivos. He answered that he learned that Hashem is everywhere. His father then stopped to ask a non-Jewish maid where G-d was. She answered: "Everywhere."

His father said: "Even a simple maid in our house knows that." The Kotzker Rebbe answered, "Before I said that Hashem is everywhere. Now I know it."

It is this conceptualization that we need to instill in our children — the idea that Hashem's presence is as real as something that we can actually visualize. The idea of making Torah concepts real is what we need to strive for. There are those who naturally give a strong sense of *ruchniyus* to their children; it is just a natural outpouring of their own being.

The first and most difficult way of doing this is that of being a *dugmah chayah* — being a role model. The Torah needs to be lived as a vehicle for potential human development, rather than Torah viewed as a heavy weight on our shoulders. Which child would choose shackles? If it is shackles to us, surely children sense this. It is difficult for parents to be introspective in this regard, as we don't want to see where we are lacking in *ruchniyus* (just as we don't want to see where our children are lacking in *ruchniyus*). Yet if our children see that we open a book of *Tehillim* when we are worried about something, or that our truest joys are those in the area of *mitzvos*, they will learn appropriate coping mechanisms in times of pain, and learn to appreciate what is truly worth being happy about.

A parent needs to stress the idea of *Hashgachah Pratis* by verbalizing it, and not keeping it to himself. In this way, the incident is elevated from the mundane, and a child's perspective on life begins to expand. How a parent responds to life is how a child learns how to respond to life.

In a negative way, many of us may have said — "When I get angry at my children, I'm not going to react as my parents did — whatever that was." Yet when under enough pressure, many of us instinctively respond by acting as we learned through our parents, though we don't want to. This just reflects the idea that our actions are making strong impressions on our children, as our parents' actions have made strong impressions on us.

Even if we find certain weaknesses in our *avodas Hashem*, our children should feel that we are consciously working to change them. This can be shown by verbalizing — "*Baruch Hashem* I *davened Minchah* today — things were so hectic — I'm glad that I was able to do it." It is helpful if a person can express his own connection to *Yiddishkeit*, and why it is important to him. If you are unable to envision a reason beyond "Well, my parents did it," you need to search within yourself for reasons with more depth. Is it possible for a spiritually impoverished parent to give a meaningful rationale for a child to remain Torah observant?

If one overvalues something not reflecting values of Torah, one's general *hashkafos* become lopsided. For example, if a parent is always only involved with thoughts of improved *gashmiyus* (be it due to a great lack of money or an over-abundance of money), a child's thoughts begin to gravitate in a similar way, either showing off her material possessions, or feeling sorry for herself, due to what she does not possess. One needs to re-evaluate values, or at the very least, don't discuss it at great lengths in front of one's children.

Another way to instill a spiritual identity in a child is to stress pride in a child's enthusiasm for a particular *mitzvah*, be it *davening*, learning, or certain acts of *chessed*, and help strengthen this enthusiasm. If a child has no inborn spiritual direction, one can help him find such a direction, and nurture this talent. A child should feel that Hashem needs him as part of the Master Plan.

In relation to schools, each school has their own approach in relation to stressing what is spiritual. Though our children's schools do impart knowledge, a slightly different way of learning and behaving is stressed each year in school, by unique and individual teachers. A consistent path of *chinuch* and integration of Torah cannot be created by the over forty uniquely different teachers that one's children may come into contact with in their years of schooling (from kindergarten until graduation). This job can only be successfully achieved by parents, who have the honesty to look at themselves and work to improve what they want to see improved in their children. Through parents' acts of sincerity in the realm of the *chinuch* of their children, and continual acts of goodness and kindness in instilling *ruchniyus* in all of Hashem's children, their children will experience (first-hand) what is most spiritual about their Torah *chinuch*.

39 *A father's involvement in chinuch*

IN CONTEMPORARY AMERICAN society a family needs to make time in order for its members to be together. Besides Shabbos, many families see little of each other throughout the week. A father may feel additional pressure to provide for his family and work extra hours to make the family more financially comfortable. However, in relation to *chinuch*, quality is often more important than quantity. Even though Torah is learned in school, parents need to reinforce the learning by stressing the values and expanding on the ideas.

This can be accomplished in five minutes at the dinner table, or between *Minchah* and *Ma'ariv* at shul. The father need not be the most outstanding *lamdan* to do this. A child will appreciate a parent who might be slow and stumbling in reading, more than a parent who makes no attempt to study at all. A father is a role model for the child, showing that one needs to participate in learning, whatever his present abilities may be. A father could make two phone calls yearly to his child's *rebbi* (besides for PTA and problems) just to show interest. This sounds like a small amount of calls, but many fathers rely on mothers for such involvement.

The word "*mesorah*" literally means to "pass down." What eternal memory can a father give to his child? The *mitzvah* of "*V'shinantam livanecha*" may be given over to teachers, but do fathers not desire a *chelek* in this special transmission? A *Gemara* in *Kedushin* speaks of a child's obligation to give remaining life-sustaining water to either his *rebbi* or his father. The child is obligated to give the water to his *rebbi* first because the *rebbi* is giving the child *Olam Haba*. However, if his father also teaches him Torah, he is obligated to give the water to his father, as his father gives him both *Olam Haba* and *Olam Hazeh*. Sons of great Rabbanim (and sons of kings many years ago) who replaced their fathers were said to "*memalei makom*" — to fill their father's place.

The idea is that, without a doubt, they learned the holy ways of their fathers and have come to an internalized knowledge of their greatness, by being with them from moment to moment. Should we feel that our sons can appreciate whatever spiritual understanding we possess? Whatever one has achieved or aspires to achieve should be given as a *yerushah* to one's children.

In relation to daughters, parents need to take *limudei kodesh* seriously if they want their daughters to take it seriously. Why should someone study for a *Chumash* test if it's not so important? Whether it's learning with one's daughter or asking questions, parents need to consider this matter. For *ruchniyus* endeavors to be paramount for women in our present society, it usually needs to be strengthened through learning. As the Chofetz Chaim foresaw many years ago (when he strongly supported Sarah Schenirer's opening of Bais Yaakov), a person (women in particular) needs to be mentally active, and the content of a person's mind is often whatever is deemed important in the home. Thus, a father's support and involvement in his daughter's learning is of paramount importance to their individual relationship, and his daughter's involvement in her Torah learning, in general.

Although in past generations much Torah was absorbed through living in a home full of *mitzvos* and *ma'asim tovim*, most families are presently not at the level of such simple osmosis and need more direct input, be it in the form of books, tapes or lectures.

As a woman is, and a girl will be, an *akeres habayis*, her family needs to validate her spiritual endeavors, not only in importance given to the secular career, if she happens to go in that direction. If importance is placed only on the secular, the whole quality and priorities in the home are significantly different. How one views oneself and one's abilities in Torah begins with one's own parental home.

Though it is easier for many men to find satisfaction with concrete results, as seen in finishing a *blatt Gemara* or in the completion of a hard day's work, there is another type of satisfaction to be experienced — becoming more involved with your child's *chinuch*. One has only to ask any child who had his or her father's involvement, what an impact it made on the child's life. The memories of this special person, who gave of what little time he had, is truly an eternal gift.

TEENAGE ISSUES

Emerging adolescent personality (Working with your teenager) 40

A S IN ALL stages of a person's life, one encounters challenges and channels for personal growth, depending on how a person perceives it. In Israel, the time of adolescence is coined "*teepaish-esray*" (or silly youth), reflecting a parent's frustration during this stage of development.

The main need for children at this point in their lives is to make a generally comfortable separation between themselves and their parents. Children need to feel a sense of sameness, but need to know where they differ from their parents, in order to appropriately define themselves as unique human beings. Clearly, no two people are exactly alike, and children need to find this delicate balance as they enter young adulthood. Finding this place takes time and much patience on the part of parents and children alike.

There is a great pressure for a teenager to "fit in" with his peers, reflecting an adolescent's need to be accepted in the "outside world." Some children are weaker by nature in relation to peer pressure, and this problem is exacerbated at the time of adolescence.

A parent needs to put more energy into the art of listening and not to stop when monosyllabic responses are given by children. A parent can share his own experiences with his child, providing an opening for a child to ask questions or express his own opinion. A parent needs to attempt to be objective, trying to understand how a child might feel a certain way (although his opinions may differ). Actually believing in a child's potential and understanding his dreams is a positive attitude that an adolescent needs to sense from his parents, as well.

If a teenager seems unhappy and his self-esteem is low, it may be part of his work of self-definition, in which he questions himself and everyone around him. This unhappiness could reflect other things, and professional help may need to be sought if the depression seems more severe.

If a parent wants to build his child's self-esteem, it would have been most preferable if it had started many years before! However, be that as it may, the process is helpful whenever it begins.

A child's opinion needs to be taken seriously and asked for in various situations. A parent can assist in developing a child's talent, or creating one (as in acts of *chassadim* to others). One can help discuss realistic goals to help give a child a sense of achievement in different areas of his life (i.e. getting up on time for school). One can display a respect for the child's maturity by showing a trust in his abilities, allowing his sense of independence and self-esteem to flourish. Allowing the child to help brainstorm solutions for a problematic situation will encourage resourcefulness in the child. Stressing a child's particular positive character traits verbally can only help a child to develop in a positive manner. Power struggles with teenagers involve much negotiation, and even writing contracts (in a simplistic non-legal fashion) have proven helpful in a number of cases.

As with all things, a person's individual *hishtadlus* in *gidul banim* (the raising of children) is limited. A person's *tefillos* become a channel to Hashem who bestows *chochmah* to parents, as most parents do not always know when to show *chessed* or *gevurah* to children, with their limited knowledge alone. For certain parents, the need to work with the "non-black and white world" of the teenager is the most challenging time of their parenting career. Thus, a person needs to *daven* for the strength and the understanding to put all constructive ideas into action to assist our children.

Teenage complaints about adult hypocrisy   41

THE INITIAL ESSENTIAL work needed to be done with adolescents who complain about adult hypocrisy is that of opening lines of communication. Being unafraid to deal with a child's discomforting thoughts and feelings is the beginning of creating a sense of mutual trust. Once a parent can clearly hear a child's problem, the work of problem-solving can begin. Families need to come together to find a way to work out problems, rather than to judge and condemn. Concrete ideas can come from such encounters, such as that of changing schools, or shuls, for a child. A parent needs to allow a child to feel loved, even though a parent presently does not agree with his actions and attitudes. If a child is simply condemned, a parent surely will only further push the child away.

In relation to a child's disappointment in seeing religious politics or seeing hypocrisy, a parent can reflect his own similar sentiments and anger towards such dishonest behavior. A parent needs to model how one can live within the disappointments and limitations of everyday life without throwing off the yoke of Torah. Such "politics" is a general human phenomenon, affecting many areas of life — not only religious areas. As the issues of jealousy, human avarice and the desire for honor push human beings away from living (as stated in *Pirkei Avos*), these human limitations affect every area of our daily existence.

Yet the *Torah Hakedoshah* itself is beyond the vessels that limited human beings may attempt to use it for. The Torah is perfect. If people do not apply its principles to their life, this does not take away its Divinity. The *mashal* can be used of that of taking a shower. Only Hashem and the human being know if soap is being used, and if the person is actually cleansing himself. The soap clearly possesses cleansing abilities. However, once a person leaves the shower, only Hashem and he know if the soap was used.

A person needs to put in great effort not to deceive himself, and not give excuses for questionable behavior. In reality, if all Jews did live up to the ideals of the Torah, our *galus* would have ended a long time ago. Our human liabilities cause all spiritual endeavors to be incomplete.

People's hypocrisies reflect human limitations. A teacher may greatly espouse the need to watch *lashon hara*, because it is one of the teacher's weak points. She may teach this (and other aspects of Torah) because she feels the teachings to be true, even though she may be lacking in this attribute.

However, if we would wait to find teachers who fully embody all principles of the Torah, we would have very few *melamdim*. It is often difficult for children — especially teenagers — to accept human limitations. A child wants to see himself as unconquerable, and cannot always accept another's limitations. A child needs to see that any society comprised of imperfect individuals is limited in its potential achievements. However, it is the Torah itself that is limitless — its comprehension and implementation of its teachings — and it is in the hand of the individual to grow within its vast waters.

In relation to the issue of power struggle, in rebellion a child may be choosing this area of his life to assert his independence. Perhaps something in the *mesorah* that a parent has transmitted to him could use more strengthening. Sometimes, a mother and father show very diverse attitudes in relation to *Yiddishkeit*, which can cause confusion in children. Thus, by rebelling, a child can be representing his state of confusion — "It's easier to reject everything than try to make sense of my parent's religious disunity." In such cases, a third, objective party can sometimes help, be it a Rav or mental health professional — in order to create more of a unified approach for a child.

It is also helpful if a parent can express his own connection to *Yiddishkeit*, and why it is important to him. If you are unable to envision a reason beyond: "Well, my parents did it," you need to search within yourself for reasons with more depth. Is it possible for a spiritually impoverished parent to give a meaningful rationale for a child to remain Torah observant?

A parent needs to help develop and strengthen her child's personal connection to *Yiddishkeit*. Be it in the area of learning a particular subject or doing particular acts of *chessed*, a child needs to feel more strongly connected. If every Jew's *neshamah* has a source in Torah, a parent needs to help find this source in her child. A child needs to eventually feel that "Hashem needs me as part of His Master Plan." The child should feel that each one of his actions is of great importance. In attempting to find this place of belonging a child's self-esteem is also enhanced as her life has definitive purpose.

Finally, a parent needs to always *daven* that her child's paths be straight, as the power of *tefillah* can never be underestimated. A person can supposedly do all the correct actions, but *emunah* can elude the heart of an angry adolescent. Trauma, such as divorce or death in the family, can cause great questioning in a child, and a parent's *tefillah* can be the greatest antidote to help avoid spiritual downfall. A Rav or a teacher who in the past may have evoked admiration from a child should be called upon for his advice and input. All sincere efforts and time spent to resolve a child's internal struggle will surely show positive results.

UNIQUE
FAMILY
UNITS

Divorce — attempting to build a "united front" with one's spouse to help create consistency for your family

42

HOW CAN ONE show this consistency after a divorce? Creating a "united front" is often mentioned in relation to mother and father — they should be seemingly united in their approach to their children. As it is said, "*k'shem she'ein shtei partzufeihem shavos*" (no two faces are alike, no two people's opinions are alike). If so, how do we deal with this reality? It is also said that a wife is an *ezer k'negdo* — a helper against him — almost like a good study partner to sharpen one's mind, and "keep him on his toes," so to speak.

These thoughts sound philosophically sound and accurate, but living them on a daily basis is a challenge for many people. According to Harav Samson Raphael Hirsch, men have a particular challenge with their sense of self, and need to prove themselves constantly. The example he cites is the fact that Adam Harishon was created from dust and will ultimately return to ashes. Since males are aware of this temporal reality, they are compelled to prove that their life (and sense of self) is essential to this world. Thus, the "male ego" differs from the female's sense of self.

A female is created from spirituality — from the rib of Adam Harishon, who is a *tzelem Elokim*. Though created from the rib — a physical part of the body — she knows her essential worth because she is created from an existing *neshamah.* Women do not generally have the need to prove their worth as continually and intensively as men do. Women were not taught Torah in an official and systemic manner until recent years, but that did not affect their spirituality throughout the many years of Jewish history.

Thus, sociologically speaking, women often capitulate to men's responses to children's issues, to avoid confrontation with their spouses. Their sense of self will usually not be altered if someone doesn't totally agree with their opinion. This is not always an optimal approach, as both parties have something to contribute, as husband and wife often complement each other.

Creating a united front results from much communication between husband and wife, where they reach some sort of common ground before issues occur. According to Rav Dessler, the root of the word *ahavah* is "*hav*" — giving. Giving (and sometimes compromising) is the way that marital love is created and maintained. One needs to analyze what is *ikar* and *tafel* (knowing one's individual priorities), in order to know what issues need to be challenged and problem-solved with one's spouse. If there are areas with major differences between husband and wife, children can pick up on this, and use one spouse against another, to have their wishes fulfilled. In simple terminology: "If Tatty says no, you can always ask Mommy."

If a couple is stuck on their differences, they should speak to a person with *da'as Torah* to get the appropriate response to the given situation. A spouse can live for years feeling inferior to his spouse, thinking that he is not religious enough, etc. Once a Rav is consulted, the issue can be clarified, and false self-flagellation can disappear. A united front is then much easier to create for one's children.

A parent could verbalize that she feels differently than her spouse in certain areas that are not of major importance. A child needs to know that parents are not carbon copies of one another. The sense of parents' similar values and responses to life is what creates the essential bonds of unity in one's home.

If parents divorce, issues of dual loyalty occur, and the issue of consistent parenting becomes more complicated. The level of amicability that exists between the divorced parents will determine whether this issue will be addressed at all. One needs to attempt to uphold general standards and visions for one's family, whether the set of parents live together or not. Whatever level of consistency is possible in unified parenting after a divorce is commendable, yet clearly difficult to achieve. Both parents need to focus on their children feeling secure, through as much consistency in their parenting direction as possible.

Whatever similarities parents shared before the divorce can be stressed afterwards, to help solidify the family strengths and unified identity. Sometimes a third party is necessary to better facilitate this process. A mutual family friend can verbally express the uniqueness of one's family — even when family members live separately — and strengthen the spiritual vision, giving the benefit of the doubt to all parties involved, to help the child to feel pride, even in a difficult situation.

Reframing problematic situations involved with divorce 43

THE PAIN OF divorce is experienced by children for many years, and reverberates through one's conscience, as does any severe change in one's life patterns and family structure. The possibility of decreasing the pain involved in this situation is a tremendous benefit that one can give to one's children, or any children going through this challenge. Initially, if one could start the divorce process with mediation, must less damage and anguish would occur, affecting all family members. Unfortunately, many people in this situation are already embroiled in anger and do not desire a more peaceable means to end their marriage, and go directly through legal systems, causing both emotional and financial stress.

Perhaps the most difficult struggle that a child experiences in this period is his eternal question: "Whose fault is it that this marriage is falling apart?" A younger child can blame himself for somehow being part of the problem — the child thinks that perhaps his misbehavior caused the parents to fight more, and it disturbed their marital harmony. A child can also blame the least-favored parent for the cause of the break-up, as this parent generally is the one to "mess things up," according to the child.

A parent needs to reframe the situation and recreate the picture to make it more workable and sane to his child. One can say to the child that, "Sometimes things are very difficult, and the most important thing is having happy mothers and fathers. Sometimes people can be happiest only when they are living apart, though it can hurt their children very much. A mother is still your mother, even if she is not living together with your father. Your father also remains your father, wherever he may live. Everything is *Hashgachah Pratis*, and everyone in this situation (for some unknowable reason) is where they are meant to be."

A child has to feel that it is okay to enjoy the company of one parent, and not feel that he is being disloyal to the other parent if he enjoys the company of the first parent. Also, one's irritation with one's ex-spouse should not get in the way of the child's relationship with his parent.

If a child thinks that either of his parents is deplorable, he might say to himself: "The acorn doesn't fall that far from the tree — how good can I possibly be?" A parent needs to foresee the far-reaching ramifications of his words and actions towards his ex-spouse, and how it will color his child's self-esteem.

When a couple makes the decision to divorce, many issues have been taken into account before coming to this point. Dealing with their children's issues is usually of paramount importance to both mother and father, but how to help look at this life change as more of a transition than a failure, takes much fortitude and inner *emunah*. If a parent mentions that *da'as Torah* was consulted before any major decisions were made, the children will know that the actions were clearly not random ones. If the parents involved were both fortunate enough to feel that all the effort possible was made to keep the marriage together, less guilt and resentment is involved when discussing this topic with their children.

When visitation with a parent is infrequent and cancellations are common, the custodial parent needs to refrain from any subjective response to his child about this sensitive matter. The custodial parent needs to give the benefit of the doubt in reference to the ex-spouse not appearing (when it is plausible and believable). This is done in order that the child's vision of himself, and his self-importance, stays intact. Again, a child may ask himself: "How good a father can I ever be, if my father acts this way to me?" In this way, the tremendous benefits of positive speech and offering the benefit of the doubt are gifts for your child — not particularly for your ex-spouse.

The art of reframing a difficult situation takes skill. Truly looking for the possible hidden good in what seems to be problematic reflects the idea that Hashem's will can sometimes be hidden. The ocean itself reflects this concept, as it reflects the *"alma diescasia"* — the sea has hidden worlds beneath its surface. In this way, a child can see that sometimes good can be hidden in painful circumstances, but each person needs to strive to see good in their own personal test.

44 Clarifying family roles in a single-parent family

THE PLIGHT OF a single parent is very difficult under any circumstances. There are multiple stresses involved, especially if a single mother is working outside the home. This adds an additional stress in relation to being able to spend time with one's children. Anyone who works many hours and returns home with strong familial needs will feel emotionally drained. Another problematic factor is that of single mothers relying on government agencies to sustain their families, causing one's family to experience a sense of poverty. Families often need to relocate after divorce — another change — often to lower conditions of housing. Possible feuds can be ongoing with an ex-spouse and in-laws, besides possible court cases.

In general, children's emotional conditions are weakened

due to events leading to single parenthood (be it illness or divorce). Doing homework with a child may be a monumental task, given the scenario described above. No person can possibly respond adequately to each and every crisis.

And yet, what is vital to attempt to create is a viable support system, consisting of relatives and close friends. A parent is validated by another adult (usually one's spouse), and grandparents' validation is not sufficient or available on a daily basis. In relation to concrete help (such as babysitting services to help create time for oneself), or places to receive adult feedback, this support system is of great importance in fortifying one's family with additional sources of strength.

In relation to older children, it may be quite difficult to maintain an authoritarian role with them, as a parent may need to often rely on her children in order to keep the house running smoothly. More teamwork is needed as an adult's help is missing. It is difficult to be called on as a responsible young adult to help, and then to be reprimanded as a child. An older son can be consciously (or unconsciously) called upon to act as "the man of the house" — be it bringing younger brothers to shul or making *Kiddush* on Shabbos. Yet later, he may be ordered around by his mother (which he finds irritating and confusing).

A way to deal with this problem is by delineating actual tasks and functions of older children. Specifying a parent's expectations clarifies a child's role, even in a more complex situation such as a single-parent family. If you need to ask a child for help, let the child's responsibilities be clear. He needs to know when he will have free time, and to generally know what is and what is not overstepping boundaries, in relation to his mother. A parent is overtly bestowing this role on her child, rather than this occurring in response to a crisis. The child is rewarded through approval and recognition, so that the parent and child can keep in mind that the child is doing a favor, rather than fulfilling a pseudo-parental obligation. This keeps the role divisions more intact.

In relation to children's mixed feelings, a strong sense of ambivalence occurs after divorce. There is a sense of divided loyalties. A child may feel: "If I'm loyal to my mother, I can't be loyal to my father." It is important to let a child know that parenthood is "non-divorceable" — both parents are his forever — and that each side of any story has validity (this includes any occurrence between his father and mother). Sometimes professional help is needed to further work with such feelings.

Divorced parents often appreciate the decrease in tension when severe marital strife no longer exists in their home. Being able to work with one opinion (instead of spouses fighting towards non-existent unity) can often strengthen families after a divorce. In time, a balance is created, if a parent consciously works on this endeavor.

45 Stepfamilies — becoming a blended family

BECOMING A BLENDED family is an all-encompassing task. To both sets of children (and to all of us), there is no complete replacement for one's natural parent. Thus, any thoughts of remarriage can bring on a sense of sadness to one's children. No stepparent has the blood tie or shared past that one's natural parent possesses. In a sense, the more a child accepts a "new parent," the more the child may feel guilty that he is betraying his natural parent (be the parent alive or deceased).

A similar sentiment can be felt on the part of a stepparent. If one's natural children are living with an ex-spouse, the stepparent can feel guilty (or less loyal) if he gives more time to his new family. The parent may feel that he is not giving enough to his natural children who are living elsewhere. A child of a deceased parent can have somewhat irrational thoughts, such as: "If you really loved Mommy, how can you marry someone else?" One could answer to the effect that: "Mommy wouldn't have wanted me to live alone, because she always wanted what's best for me."

In reality, children see stepparents as a relief or a threat, depending on their position in the family. For some "parentified children" (those that temporarily made *Kiddush* for the family, or cooked much of the family meals), there is a definite change in status (there is another person in an authoritative position to be dealt with). For other children, there is discomfort in having a stranger in the house. Some reconstituted families have to move into the homes of their step-siblings, having to usurp territory and create new roles in a pre-existing family. Children that took on more parental roles in recent years need to rediscover their original "child" roles, when two parents work together. It is quite natural to have mixed feelings when so much transition is in the making.

Creating blended families is a tenuous process. Care and attention needs to be given to all parameters of the situation. In more common situations, at least nine months needs to pass from entering the role of spouse to entering the role of parent. When creating a blended family, adults become spouses and parents simultaneously. In this case, the parent-child relationship precedes the marital relationship, so that the past ties have different weight and meaning in the family. Not only this, but each child enters this family unit suffering from a loss. People may have learned well (or not) how to deal with disappointment. How comfortably one acclimates to this change is dependent on how one's coping mechanisms function.

The initial step that one needs to take is that of solidifying one's marital relationship at the onset of the marriage. If this does not occur, a woman can become only a housekeeper and mother, not necessarily a wife. A person can come to feel resentful, and could actually emerge somewhat like the mythical stepmother.

The myth of instant love is equally faulty. One needs time to develop relationships, including making set times to get to really know one's stepchildren (instead of merely meeting over the breakfast table). Both parents need to work as a unit in relation to their children. Although in the past, one parent and her children was a unit, restructuring of roles in the family needs to occur in order to include and validate a new parent. In this way, one can strengthen the relationship with one's stepchildren and help solidify both parents' authority in the family.

Putting together the experiences of two different families is quite a challenge and requires work to weave the tapestries of life together. Yet many have succeeded in enriching their lives by remarriage and all people's experiences can be growth-producing, when shared in a constructive and positive manner.

ADDENDUM:

PRACTICAL
HELPFUL
FAMILY IDEAS

Choosing a school for your child 46

WHEN A PARENT embarks upon the challenging journey of choosing an appropriate school for her child, many questions arise that require a response. The first step necessary in getting to know a school is to speak to its parent body. If one happens to speak to a parent who is totally satisfied with everything in the school, one needs to speak to another parent (as any responsible parent would do this in relation to a *shidduch* for their child, as well). Though a person can marry many people's good points, we have a more difficult time tolerating others' particular negative qualities. The same applies to schools. We may be very satisfied with a school's positive accomplishments, but find ourselves unable to live easily with certain of its liabilities. Meeting a principal is helpful, because a principal reflects the direction of the school and what its priorities are. A principal's directives affect the top teaching staff, down to the role of the janitor, as all employees desire to satisfy their employer.

When researching a school it is important to keep in mind what its student body is like. Are the families similar to your family — be it in relation to the degree of religious observance, financial situation, or cultural similarities? A child needs to fit in as much as possible to avoid unnecessary discomfort and stress.

In relation to the level of religious observance, if one needs to choose a school whose religious level differs from one's family, it is preferable to choose a level which is higher rather than lower. Children may be embarrassed if they are more religious than most of their class, and may hide behavior which classmates may deem to be extreme. However, if a school's students are somewhat more observant, a child can either choose to go in that direction or not, as long as the student body is not judgmental or condescending. If students are judgmental, being different can be quite uncomfortable as well, in these circumstances.

In general, creating and maintaining friendships is of paramount importance to many female students and this issue cannot be minimized. If possible, one needs to get a sense of a child's actual potential class and parent body in order to appropriately assess the situation.

While social issues are very important to female students, academic challenges are most central to male students. Boys' self-esteem usually is more connected to a sense of competition and the desire to be motivated and to achieve. (Thus, there is a great problem with male students who find it difficult to perform academically.) Boys have less extra-curricular activities during a given yeshivah schedule and more emphasis falls on the academic alone. Thus, when looking for a school for boys, the academic is essential. If a child has learning problems, or particular school needs, ways to deal with these issues need to be acknowledged and agreed upon with the administration, in order for the school to be a desirable placement. The actual amount of students in a class reflects the amount of individual attention any student can realistically expect to receive. This, too, needs to be taken into consideration when choosing a school.

If a parent actually finds a school and there is no opening available, one needs to attempt to speak to another parent in the school or a school board member, to help accelerate this process. We live in an imperfect world, and one needs to advocate for one's child in whatever way is possible.

However, sometimes parents' choices are very limited due to the limited actual options available. Parents may desire that their children attend a school which reflects their particular ideology or group identification. In such a case, only one school alone can often exist in a given Jewish community. Another example of this "one school phenomenon" is when a family is living in an out-of-town, small community. In the above-mentioned cases, where one's actual school choices are limited, individual parental input into the child's education may be possible, depending upon the attitude of the school's administration. In this area, choices in education are more geared to affecting the quality of education, rather than choosing an institute itself.

In truth, one needs to *daven* that one's child can reach his potential in learning and in all areas, as we can only attempt to make the best decisions for our children. All the efforts made in this direction can be sensed by children at various stages in their lives, and hopefully this devotion will help them to develop properly in all ways and to continually improve in all areas.

Creative ways to spend time with your child — quality time in moments 47

PARENTS OFTEN SPEAK of attempting to create quality time for their children, and wonder how to create this island of oasis in a crowded twenty-four hours. This island often never exists. Yet instead of being in continual regret about this reality, it is preferable to attempt to make a make-shift "quasi" island of time with one's children, and accept life's limitations. A parent can make a fifteen-minute spontaneous trip to the ice-cream store into an expedition to the North Pole, with a humorous story and an imaginative mind. When one walks together with a child to a pediatrician, one can quietly sing a song together that they both like, and share. A parent can use carpool time as quality time with her child. When your child is the last remaining one in the car, you can say: "This is our special time in the carpool together." By verbalizing that this is your time together, it becomes its own special moment in time. A parent is not on the cell phone, and does not mention test grades, or topics of pressure, in these few moments. A parent can sing a child's favorite song together with her child, or a song that they both know from a children's tape. A child can feel very loved and treasured by a parent in these precious moments.

A child's positive childhood memories need not be a trip to the amusement park or a prolonged hotel stay. Most positive childhood memories are those associated with relaxed and happy parents and siblings, and these settings often vary. Warm feelings of sharing time and love can be in simple places and simple moments. As we elevate time and space by our *mitzvos*, we can also elevate the parent/child bond, by sanctifying time in a most profound and spiritual relationship.

48 Short-term positive-reinforcement techniques

THE TWO MAIN positive parenting factors that have proven to be essential in creating well-balanced children are that of a parent showing consistency in parent/child interactions and a parent showing some type of positive reinforcement, in her parenting interactions. The problem that most parents encounter is that reinforcement systems involving charts are short in duration, due to a child's losing interest. Statistically speaking, these charts usually last for a maximum of three weeks (often depending on the endurance and consistency of the parents), and new motivational techniques need to be introduced to keep the momentum alive. Translated into daily parent vernacular, most of us lose interest ourselves, once the system is not working as successfully as it was in its beginning stages.

One type of reinforcement system that includes more variety and more built-in room for success is one that deals with a variety of goals and all levels of possible rewards. Such a positive reward system involves three sheets of paper for each child — 1) One sheet has the child's name on it and the amount of points that she may accrue, 2) The next sheet has a few possible goals for the child to achieve, ranging from easy goals to more difficult ones, and 3) The final sheet has a list of rewards that the child has chosen, and points written down to achieve these rewards.

The advantage of such a system (rather than the usual one-goal chart) is that a child need not wait a long month and lose interest. This method allows for a variety of rewards and children may modify or change them with the parent's approval. These charts reflect a child's way of accepting responsibility for her actions and achievements. Though a few days may pass where a child may lose interest, the interest picks up when different rewards are suggested. This system works for most ages, but requires more sophisticated motivational ideas for older children.

GENERAL RULES:

The rewards chosen by the child can be time spent playing a game with a parent on Shabbos or a trip to a museum, when enough points are accumulated. A parent has to have the prerogative from the start to change the amount of points initially chosen, if it goes too slowly or too quickly. A child never feels that he is a failure, as he can always get a piece of gum for remembering to wash *negel vasser*, etc.

This reflects a concept in *avodas Hashem*, found in the teachings of Reb Nachman of Breslov. Referring to the words of *Tehillim*: "I sing to Hashem *bodi*" — with the little that is remaining within me. Reb Nachman explains the plight of humankind and how people so easily give up on themselves. He questions how one is able to pick oneself up and begin again in his *avodas Hashem*. One has to recall the day's activities, and "re-envision" whatever *mitzvos* one may have gathered, however insignificant they may seem in their own eyes. "Did I not say *Modeh Ani* when I was half asleep?" "Did I not refrain from yelling at my daughter for taking my slippers?" In this way, we gather together our *nekudos tovos* (good points) that initially may seem small. Yet this thinking has a snowball effect upon us, as each positive action convinces us that we can do even more. We believe that we are still capable of serving Hashem, whatever our limitations may seem to be.

In a similar vein, such a positive-reinforcement system capitalizes on the same concept. "Perhaps I was unable to be successful in not teasing my sister, but I did my homework on time, and was rewarded for that with a piece of bubble gum. I guess I can still be 'okay' in other ways. And I did *daven Minchah* without being reminded." A child is very clear that he is not being rewarded for teasing his sister. For such a challenging goal the amount of points is much greater. The bubble gum is a reward for a simpler positive action. If a child engages in a more severe negative behavior, however, the reward for the simpler behavior is still received, but at a later time.

In the same way that we would want to be rewarded for our positive actions, and not lose credit for what we did appropriately, so the same holds true for our children. If we complete a project at work in a very timely and superior fashion, we may receive a bonus from our employer. We would feel cheated if that bonus was retracted, after coming to work late two days in a row. If we need to be docked from pay for coming late, this is understandable. Yet if we received a monetary bonus for superior work, let us feel proud of our achievements. Let this motivate us to go forward in this direction. In the same way, a parent should not take away points at any given time. If a child needs a consequence for a negative behavior this is understandable, but not at the risk of losing hard-earned points. In this way, as Reb Nachman relates, one can truly sing to Hashem *b'odi* — with the little good that is remaining with me. That little good can be transformed into much greatness.

In this way, he can receive many points for many small activities, which helps him to acquire a belief in himself, while he gains the ability to tackle the more-difficult challenges.

Exciting and challenging positive-reinforcement techniques 49

O<small>N A SIMPLISTIC</small> level, there are various other ways to create unique positive-reinforcement methods. One can use a timer with children, and attempt a home-made version of "Beat the Clock." When the timer rings, the job has to be complete. Somehow the challenge of an outside monitor motivates children — especially because it is non-human — by taking away the issue of human power struggle that one usually encounters with an authority figure.

Counting down from twenty to zero is also a technique that is very helpful, especially for bedtime issues. One needs to use one's techniques without anger and apparent irritation, to avoid entering a power struggle with one's children. In a power struggle, both sides desire to win, and one needs to attempt to be a role model of negotiation and calm, to avoid such situations.

One can make undesirable jobs more workable by using some creativity. On Erev Pesach you can have children clean the walls with squirt cans, if they are able to be part of your cleaning crew. One child pretends that she is a mother when she cleans the kitchen, and prefers to be alone in this endeavor as she enters this imaginative world (which would otherwise have been very tedious).

One can create a family project and when it is complete all members can participate in an outing to the neighborhood ice-cream store. One can also break down seemingly gigantic jobs into smaller components. (This is also of help to adults!) Sometimes a fifteen-minute work period followed by a short break can make a long job more bearable. It is also important to remember that a child needs to feel successful in the job that she does. Let the child make her bed (even if it is not to your liking), to help build her sense of competency. A parent can improve on it after the child leaves, but at least the child feels her work was acceptable. The appreciation experienced both behaviorally and verbally is positive reinforcement in itself.

Davening — the 50th gate 50

T HERE IS A *midrash* that states the importance of *daven-ing*, and its effect upon each person's life. It is said that if Moshe Rabbeinu had made one more *tefillah*, he would have been given permission to enter Eretz Yisrael, and the *gezeirah* would have been nullified. A person never knows the effect of her *tefillos* and requests for *siyatta diShmaya*.

In general, in all of our endeavors (particularly in the area of parenting), one needs to *daven* for *siyatta diSh-maya*, because each one of our parenting circumstances differ. What may be effective for one child when they are nine years old may not be effective at age eleven. It is writ-ten that *"haba l'taher mesayin oso"* — when we approach Hashem to purify ourselves, we are assisted in the process. We should continue to *daven* to see clearly in difficult situations and to be able to make constructive decisions in these circumstances. Through this clearer vision, may we be able to spread goodness and kindness, making the world a more spiritually elevated environment in order to receive Moshiach imminently.

About the Author

SHIRA FRANK, LCSW, has been a social worker for over thirty years, and resides with her husband and children in Flatbush, in Brooklyn, NY. Mrs. Frank's areas of specialization include family therapy, play therapy and parent training, and she has worked in private practice for over twenty years. Mrs. Frank also supervises mental health professionals extensively, and speaks publicly on various issues of mental health and Jewish philosophy. She has published over eighty articles on topics of self-help and Jewish philosophy, and her CDs are available in Judaica stores in the metropolitan-New York area. She is a featured lecturer on Kol Halashon, where she presents eighteen classes on topics of marital issues and child-rearing. She can be reached at shirafranklcsw@gmail.com.